Dedication

This book is dedicated to all those contributors and volunteers, dead or alive, who are not mentioned here but who nonetheless, freely contributed and continue to contribute in one way or another to make the Rotunda Church what it is today.

Preface

There is probably no known area in the world that holds as many churches, chapels and Neolithic temples in its territory as the tiny island of Gozo.

The Ġgantija megalithic temple predates the Pyramids of ancient Egypt by some 1,500 years and is considered to be one of the oldest freestanding temples in the world.

In order to understand and appreciate better how the monumental Rotunda Church of Xewkija came to be, this guide is an eye-witness account of what actually happened during and after the construction of this mightily impressive church, that defied skeptics and critics.

Rarely had such an impoverished village of a little more than 3,000 inhabitants built such a grand monument. Rarely had human motivation seemed more determined.

It is a faithful testimony of the history, the evolution and the remarkable construction of this magnificent Roman Catholic church that dominates the skyline of the island.

Furthermore, it attests to the indomitable spirit, unfailing courage, sheer perseverance and the remarkable skill of the villagers, the *Xewkin*.

The outstanding Rotunda is the result of a long series of planning, hard work, and tremendous sacrifice. It had to contend with natural and accidental vicissitudes over the course of two decades, throughout which spread the construction of this church.

This great photo by pioneer George Grech was submitted in an international competition under the title of 'Heaven's Support'. George used a Rolleicord III with a lens, diaphragm opening f:11 and an exposure of 1/25 sec. using an F.P.3 Rollfilm November 1953

Suffice it to say that an exceptional number of patterns were required to design and cut down the size of the stone. Some 1,600 patterned designs (*mollijiet*) were devised for this purpose.

The incredible role played by the *Xewkin*, particularly the scores of volunteers was no less significant. Without these generous men and women, the Rotunda could not have been built in just two decades.

The noble architecture of this building, inspired by an archpriest with a passion for construction, leaves memories that linger for years.

It is fair to state that the principal master stone masons who led the way are now regarded as three of the very best on the Maltese islands.

No part of the complex architectural structure or the collection of paintings and sculptured stones that complete it is casual.

Every stone, with its sculpted or carved decoration, has its meaning and justification, within a structure that was carefully studied by its sublime architect, Giuseppe D'Amato, also known as Ġuże'.

It is remarkably executed to an order of calculated perfection with geometrical designs, giving life to a downright monumental church, by its three indomitable master stone masons, Ġużepp Cauchi, Toni Vella and Ġużepp Vella.

The choice of pure globiġerina limestone, locally known as *il-ġebla tal-franka*, makes it an unparalleled monument of Gozo's artistic and cultural history, an imposing sacred church of outstanding richness and unrepeatable beauty.

Each visitor entering the Rotunda is rapt in awe at the vision of eight, beautiful proportionate columns, on which the 45,000- tons dome sits.

More than a building, it is a mirror and weave of an idyllic island. It is a faithful exaltation and reminder of its incomparable destiny, a glory of modern architecture.

With an almost absolute supremacy, so immensely rising above the skies, reaching towards heaven, with its two imposing domes, one mightier than the other, the Rotunda proclaims far and wide that this is indeed a temple of God.

Foreword

*Ix-xita traxxax ħesrem hekk kif dalam
Anna bdiet titriegħed tant bil-bard
Il-logħob tar-rummy fil-kwiet kien dak li fadal
Waqt li Luke jaħasra jissielet kontra l-mard.*

*Il-ħoss ta' trakk għaddej f'Triq il-Ħamrija.
Skoss nagħaġ ma' ragħaj jimirħu fuq bankina.
Bla televixin, tpaċpaċ u tilgħab filgħaxija.
U żjara lil Mulej għal quddiesa u tqarbina.
Il-gass jillikja mill-cooker ta' Marija
Dan huwa l-gost u s-seher tax-Xewkija.*

Freely translated into English as follows:

As it grew dark, the rain started falling.
Feeling cold, Anna started shivering.
Nothing else to do but play rummy.
While poor Luke bravely fights his cold.

A truck could be heard driving along Soil Street.
A bunch of sheep, and their shepherd, navigating the pavement
No TV, so we play and chat through the evening,
And visit God for mass and communion.
Maria's cooker is leaking gas.
This is the fun and magic of Xewkija.

Feeling inspired, I wrote this poem, in its Maltese rhyming version, on April 1, 1997. My wife Anna, along with James and Luke, our two (then young) sons aged 12 and 6, and I were spending some quality time in frugal surroundings: a semi-furnished ground-floor flat in Soil Street, Xewkija, rented from our good friend Marija Grech ta' Bejża, enjoying our annual Gozo getaway in the week after Easter. Looking back, these were special times: so many adventures on those Gozo escapes, including – on this occasion – power cuts, leaking gas, bad weather, and a bout of ill health. What else could go wrong?

And yet...There was, there is something about Xewkija that continues to allure me. An elusive je ne sais quoi that has whiffs of nostalgia, authenticity and rusticity, even though, as a critical social scientist, I am more than aware that much of this suite of features may be my own construction, a figment that has been willed into existence to satisfy my own expectations of a successful holiday. But then, it is surely not just a fanciful invention of a single mind: Xewkija was – is – a human and physical community that has inspired some deep relationship in our lives; Anna and I connected intimately with people there, even though we would only see them and talk to them for a few days, and then not again until twelve months or so later. These included Maria, her son Ġanni and his wife Anna; Saminu the baker; our friends Joe and Rosemarie Azzopardi and their two daughters, living at ta'Ġokk. I guess many Maltese, hopeless aficionados of the island of Gozo like myself, would have similar warm feelings of the place: redolent with meaning and affect.

Part of our daily ritual while in Xewkija was to go to evening mass in the Rotunda that is the subject of this book. The building is an icon of the local community that built it in the first place; a living testimony of faith as much as sheer hard work and collective effort.

I was introduced to the story of Xewkija and its church while reading a master's degree in development studies in The Hague, the Netherlands, in 1985-86. One of our professors, a Dutchman by the name of Gerard Kester, had been a regular visitor to Malta, and he thought fit to refer to the Xewkija Rotunda in the introduction to one of his courses. I was taken completely by surprise: here I was, the only Maltese student at the Institute, and suddenly the majestic product of the toil, sweat and savings of so many Gozitan workers is referred to as one clear example of collective participation. We were then cogently reminded that people can cooperate in pursuit of a cause they strongly believe in and that not everything that people do is done for material gain.(Marija ta' Bejża was one such embodiment, always on the go, organizing lotteries and events, and with all proceeds going to the Church.) Two ideas are worth keeping in mind in this individualistic and consumer-driven age.

I am grateful to Ted Mizzi for putting pen, and photos, to paper, regaling us with this book, a rich testimonial to the people of Xewkija, past, present and future.

Godfrey Baldacchino

Professor of Sociology, University of Malta, Malta
Island Studies Teaching Fellow, University of Prince Edward Island, Canada
Visiting Professor of Island Tourism, Universita' di Corsica Pascal Paoli, France
Executive Editor, Island Studies Journal
President, ISISA (International Small Islands Studies Association)

A word of thanks

A factual book is probably never written by oneself, and this one is no exception. I am indebted to more than a few resourceful and generous persons for their assistance, over a period of more than two years, in collecting and verifying the facts.

The deepest gratitude goes to Max Xuereb, a professional photographer who immediately and without reservation, accepted to shoot, *senza interessi*, many of these great photos displayed here.

By cataloguing on CD all the other priceless photographs retrieved from the Parish archives, and other private collections, Max Xuereb will long be remembered for this achievement and the handing down of the legacy of these photos to posterity.

I would also like to thank Prof. Godfrey Baldacchino for graciously accepting to write the introduction; all the clergy of Xewkija, dead and alive; Archpriest Emeritus Mgr. Carmelo Mercieca and the assistant pastor Dun Ġorġ Mercieca for their time and help and in allowing me unlimited access to the archives; my brother the assistant pastor Dun Ġwann Mizzi, for browsing hundreds of pages and choosing all those pertaining to the Rotunda; Benny Mercieca and Dun Edward Xuereb for reading the draft copy; my dear wife Vivienne and my precious daughter Francesca for their invaluable assistance; my nephew, Anthony P.Mizzi for listing the book online; Edward Farrugia from Progress Press, Ray Grima and the late Albert Pearson from MPS for their patience and counsel; the pioneer photographer George Grech *tal-Ħawwiefa* of Grech Studio, Rabat, who were the official photographers when Bishop Ġużeppi Pace laid the foundation stone, as well as for the precious photos found in the Parish archives related to the construction of the Rotunda; the Mayor Paul Azzopardi, for always being there when needed; Randu Zammit *ta' Randu* from Żebbuġ, and Joseph Camilleri from Xagħra, for sharing their private photo collection; Chevalier Paul Camilleri Cauchi for the artist's impression of the Megalithic temple of *Maqgħad ix-Xiħ*; Pawlu Pace *tal-Balakk*, the totally dedicated sacristan who made things so much easier even during unholy hours; George Schembri for kindly lending his super-high lift, gratis, to take the photos from inside the church; Perit Joseph Mizzi, my cousin Joe Xerri *ta' Xmun*; Ġuża Vella *tal-Malla*; Feliċ Spiteri *tal-Pisklu*, Ġużepp Pace *ta' Pawla*, and many others who are too numerous to mention here, but who all jogged my memory when it was failing.

Almost everything in this book is based on my experience as I was growing up and living in this old village, the first one to be formed as such in the countryside of Gozo. I hope this work is free of stereotypes and clichés. If this is present, then it is simply because I have found that it is so.

The intention of this book is not to be an academic work. Rather, it is more of a personal guide to share with an outsider. It is an education, sociological observation if you will, an interpretation of the history, events, customs, traditions, habits, values, and the strong beliefs of a community.

Moreover, it is intended to lay bare the unique character of a people that have contributed in one way or another to see this monument become a reality.

It is a remarkable journey from a Megalithic temple to the present Rotunda Church, a journey where we meet several outstanding individuals who were determined to make it happen.

Finally, special thanks go to you dear reader, by acquiring this book, from which all proceeds will go towards the continuously related expenses and maintenance of an inestimable treasure, the marvelous Rotunda Church.

Credits:

All of the old photos (particularly those in black & white) contained in this book were digitally scanned from the Xewkija Parish Archive at The Photoshop, gratis. Similarly, the new pictures (color) were all taken by Max Xuereb unless otherwise indicated.

This publication is made possible by a grant from ***firstgozo.com***

THE ROTUNDA
A TESTAMENT TO FAITH, COURAGE, AND LOVE

Text by
    Ted M. Mizzi

Photographic references
    Max Xuereb
    Xewkija Parish Archive

Editing and Design
    MPS Marketing Communications Ltd

Pagesetting
    Faraxa Publishing

Proofreading
    Francesca M. Mizzi

Listing online
    Anthony P. Mizzi
    Faraxa Publishing

Cover
    Max Xuereb
    The Rotunda Church
    Xewkija

Printed in the United States

First Edition
    November 2015

© Ted M. Mizzi, 2015

All rights reserved. No part of this publication may be reproduced, stored in a retrieval system, or transmitted in any form or by any means without prior permission of the Publisher.

ISBN 978-99957-0-874-0

Index

Preface	v
Foreword	vii
A word of thanks	ix
Neolithic times and early history - from first settlers to post war life	1
From paganism to christianity	19
The first village parish	25
It takes a village (and one shilling)	39
A born genius	55
Golden ring	73
The dome	89
Beyond the Rotunda	105
Shepherding the flock	127
End note	154
Art and architectural terms used in this guide	157
Essential bibliography and sources	160

Chapter One

Neolithic Times and Early History
From First Settlers to Post War life

"He who cannot draw on three thousand years is living from hand to mouth."
                                    Johann Wolfgang von Goethe

I had rather one day in your temple than a thousand elsewhere.
                                    Psalm 64

Before the construction of the Rotunda, before the first chapel of 1575 named after St. John the Baptist, this area was known as *Maqgħad ix-Xiħ* or as *Maqgħad ix-Xejk*. It is the throne of the village headman while later on it was more commonly known as *iċ-Ċens ta' San Ġwann*, that is, the Fief of Saint John.

Up to the 17th century, remains of an imposing Neolithic temple could be seen on the site where there is the Rotunda today, in the form of a huge dolmen. It consisted of a flat 4.5 meters (15 feet) block resting on four upright megaliths 1.6 meters (5$^{1/2}$ feet) high and which possibly derive from the entrance structure of the temple.

Giovanni Francesco Abela (1582 -1655) in his book 'Malta Illustrata' published in 1647, states that, "one could still see a big obelisk/pillar (monolith) that could measure more than 16ft."

Abela goes on to say that these huge stones were pulled down and used for the foundations of the second parish church in 1667. Others were split up into smaller parts by a tenant farmer to build a rubble wall in his field.

Other massive stones, one of them a menhir measuring 7.6 meters (25feet), is still buried under the soil as part of the foundations in 1745. Gozitan historian Agius de Soldanis also stated that the foundations of the church included huge blocks similar to those of the megalithic temples.

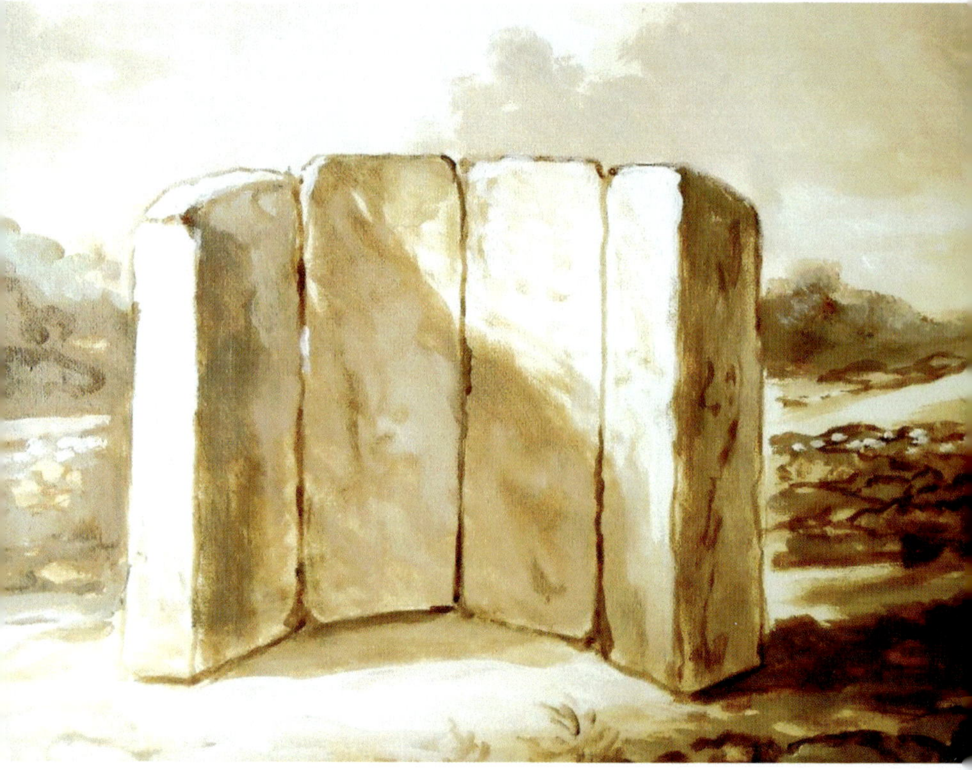

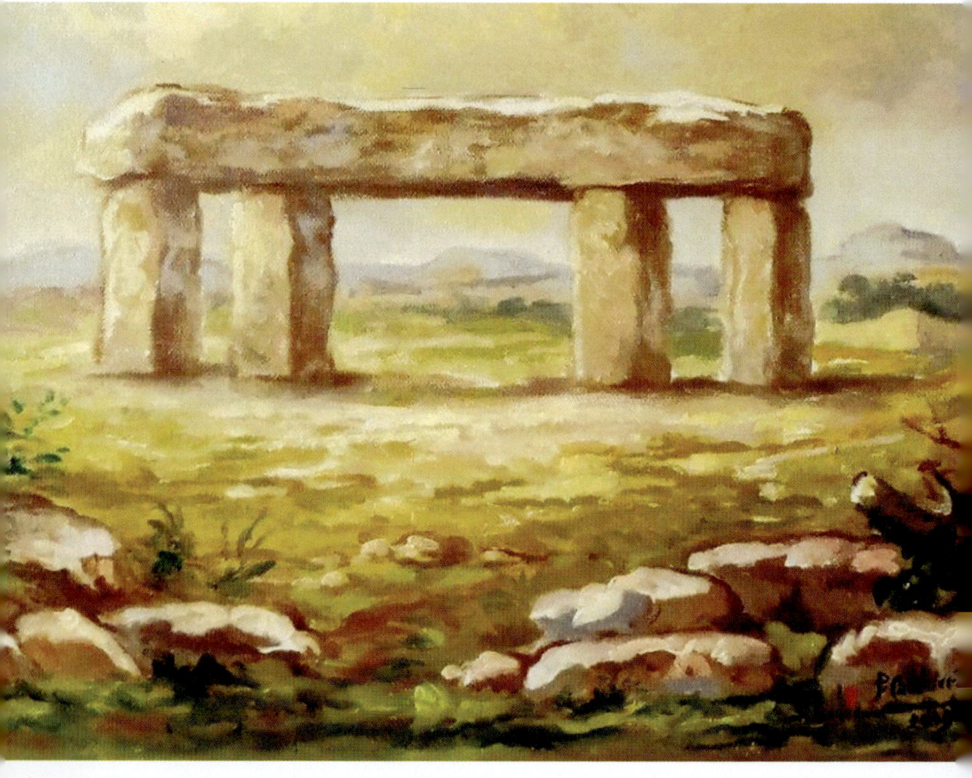

This was confirmed when parts of the prehistoric structure were unearthed in 1972. It happened when the foundations of the ornate Baroque Museum of Sculpture that are adjoining the Rotunda and housing Rococo sculpture from the old church were pulled down to make space for the new church.

In 1906, Father Emmanuel Magri, a Jesuit ethnographer and archeologist, published 'A First Report: Ruins of a Megalithic Temple at Xeuchia (Shewkijah) Gozo'.

Most interesting is how Father Magri opens his 'First Report': *"1. Xeuchia (Shewkiyah) is situated on an eminence between the Rabat main road and the great geological fault, facing the S.W. cliffs of Gozo. Its inhabitants claim for their village the honour of having been the seat of the first settlers in the island of Gozo. They still point out the caves where their chief (esh-shiekh) administered justice and had culprits kept in custody. "Għar ish-shiekh" and "el-Habs" are natural caves on the top of the table-land overlooking Wied Ħanzirah and Mgiarr ix- Xini (Mjarr esh-Shini). Il- Ħabs is very deep and sinuous"*.
Father Magri mentions the remains of large stones buried in the ground.

He goes on to state, *"Plans of the above mentioned seat of the chief have been seen in the possession of the late Dr. Lewis Bondi of Rabat by persons still alive. They describe the structure as composed of four pieces of huge stones, forming a sort of niche"*.

After clearing the topsoil, he found the remains of pottery sherds and other artifacts, including a rare footed bowl with incised designs. This bowl is today on display at the Gozo Museum of Archaeology.

Before he could continue with his trial excavations, Father Magri died a year later in Sfax, Tunisia where he had gone to preach Lenten spiritual exercises and celebrate Easter with the Maltese community over there.

For many children, including the present writer and particularly those hailing from around the village square, and the immediate area of San Bert, *ić-Ċens*, was a common venue. Here we passed much time happily playing and hanging around.

Artist's impression of the megalithic temple by Chevalier Paul Camilleri Cauchi.

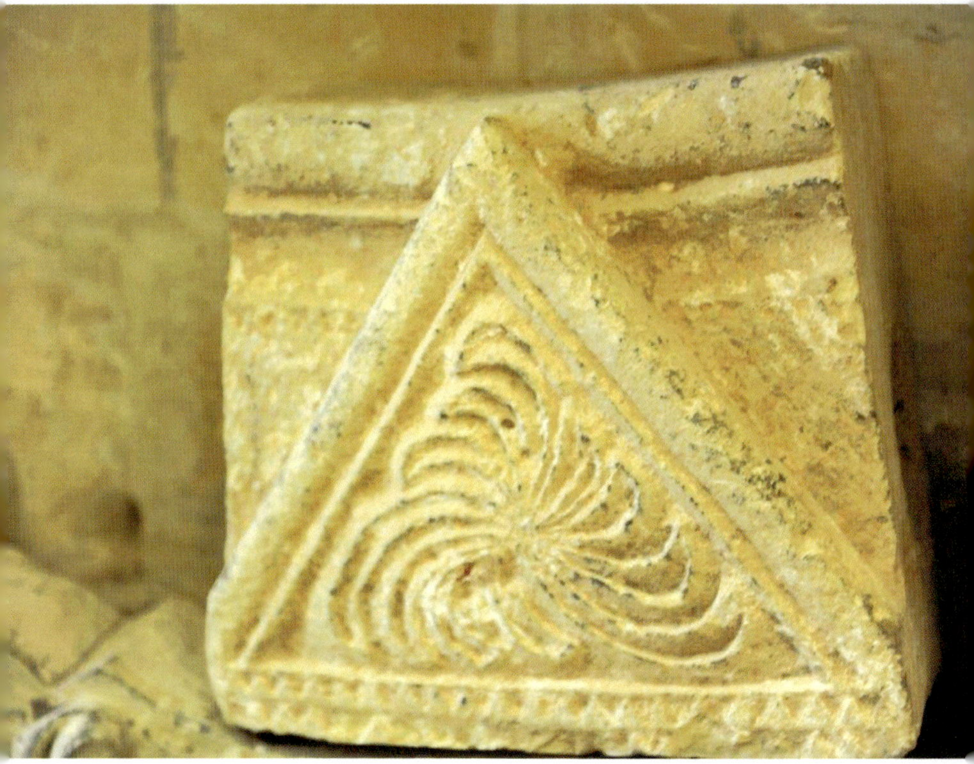

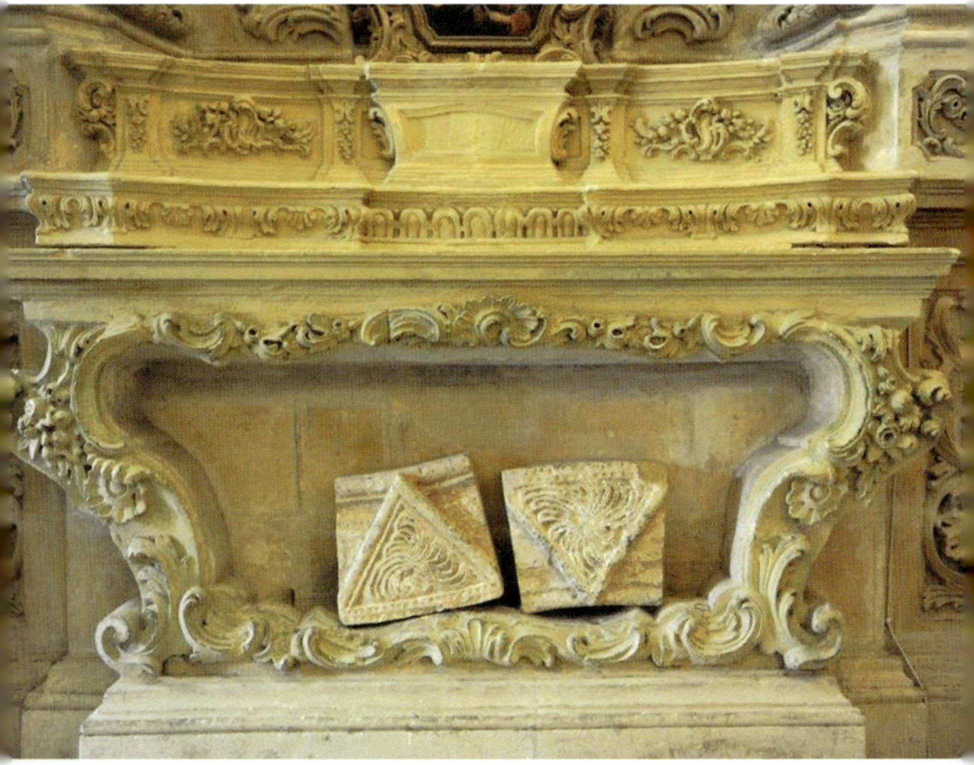

This area consisted of a large garigue enclave with rubble-strewn fields divided by low, dry stone walls. This locality practically served as our unofficial playing field. We did not have much choice, either and considered ourselves lucky to have this bit of land to kick a ball around.

We searched for the Tangier pea *qrempuċ*, trapped sparrows and played football. Other children tended their family's sheep and goat herds. The feast's petards were hoisted here as well.

In this wide open space, the stones carried on the truck of the contractor *ta' Randu*, for the building of the Rotunda were unloaded. These were left here until finding their final destination in the edifice of the new church.

Sometimes, the size of the stone delivered was so huge, that *ta' Randu* had to load and carry just one single stone block in the truck from his quarry in the village of Għarb to Xewkija.

Three of five enigmatic stones unearthed at *Maqgħad ix-Xiħ*, exhibited at the Museum of Sculpture

Since the truck had no hydraulics to unload, the stone was tied with a strong rope and pulled down with the help of many children after school hours. These children were organized into a sort of game called "pull."

The stone landed on a bed of fine talcum-like powder stone dust, locally referred to as *rina*, which is obtained from the quarry itself when the stone is cut. This stone dust is then sieved and mixed with water until it becomes slushy so that the mason can build the stones on each other.

Many times children used to play hide and seek beneath these gigantic toppled limestones, some weighing over 3 tons, many the size of a dining table. In one such game, a four-year-old boy was hidden inside the bowl of a small Benford cement mixer. Children would return home caked with stone dust.

Whole afternoons were spent down trekking deep in the valley of Mġarr ix-Xini with my friend Ninu Hili, looking along the watercourse for the rare *anżilor*. It is a type of wild red berry amongst a bed of karstic garigue and maquis vegetation.

Brown, empty desert dry fields turned into bright green carpets with the first rain of the season, making an ever-changing quilt of color and texture. Later, wildflowers blossomed and ran riot all over the countryside.

The valley is one of the deepest and most difficult and dangerous to cross on the island. It is a natural breeding ground for several species of birds including the highly prized Peregrine Falcon, the elusive Blue Rock-Thrush (the national bird of Malta), the Jackdaw and the now sadly extinct Barn Owl.

The nests that we came across were those of the ubiquitous Spanish Sparrows or Sardinian Warblers or the *Bilbla*, the Lark or the *Durrajsa*, the Rustic Bunting (*Emberiza rustica*).

The latter has a beautiful melancholic song, particularly at dusk, as the sun starts fading away and slowly disappears into the abyss of the sea beyond the horizon. As the gentle breeze dies down, and the rustling of azaleas stops, then the stillness of the countryside is almost complete.

We would count the eggs or the hungry, crying chicks that had just been hatched, laying in their cozy nest and make a mental note to come back and inspect them later on. However, we hardly ever did.

From time to time a gun shot rang out and shattered the tranquil air, as the echoes of the gunfire reverberated loudly across the deep, insidious valley. Avid hunters would pursue their game doggedly and cross over to the mighty cliffs of ta' Ċenċ.

Other fearless hunters would abseil, strapped to their waist with just a thin rope down the sheer, perpendicular cliffs over the dark ink blue waters, looking for the Peregrine's nest.

The wied was then extremely rich in biodiversity with a riot of exotic wild plants. It was easy to come upon the rare Cage Thistle or the Spanish Broom or the lovely native plant *Papoċċi*, the Baby Snapdragon (botanic name *linaria pssuedolaxifora*) with its delicate pink and red petals. Many of these plants are endemic and restricted to the Mediterranean region.

Between the numerous shrubs and indigenous scented

flowers and plants like the anise, we would climb the steep-sided creek of *Għar ix-Xiħ*. We made our way home inebriated, across verdant fields and ancient dry rubble walls, pulling and eating the fragrant tender stalks of the red crimson clover or the sweet pods of carob trees.

Ninu loved blackberries. He would crave and talk about the flavor, size and ripeness of blackberries all winter long. And so, in the blazing hot afternoon summer sun, we would enthusiastically bicycle all the way down to the wied ta' Xħajma.

This lush and green valley has a watercourse where frogs breed in the streams near the fallow fields. Rivulets flanked fertile apple orchards and meandered down to Ramla Bay and the open Mediterranean sea. We would climb the centuries old two-storey high mulberry trees like agile monkeys and make a veritable feast of swollen-ripe glossy black berries. If one of the branches had to give way under our weight, we were certainly doomed.

However, Ninu was right. These were some of the most delicious, plump and juiciest blackberries in the whole world. Blackberrying remained a special outing on our summer calendar and a uniquely rewarding leisure activity.

It was a time when children had no Xbox, tablet or PlayStation, mobile, Wi-Fi or iCloud. Most households had running water and electricity, but no refrigerators or washing machines. These basic appliances had not arrived yet in our village.

Owning a good photo camera was for the professional or the well-heeled.We were the last generation that grew up without television. The digital age was still light years away.

Paupers had to stand in line to fetch water from the mains supplied by the local government and provided at specific points on public roads.

Once, a girl in her enthusiasm jumped the queue. She was rapidly hit in the head with an iron pail, most certainly in a fit of rage, at best, in a momentary lapse of reason, by another person waiting in the scorching sun. Sadly, as a consequence of the force of the blow, the young girl lost

MEGALITHIC RUINS
XEUCHIA - GOZO.
R ELLIS

8 - The Rotunda

Rubble walls
built from
Megalithic Ruins -
Notice the Cross
engraved on the
third stone both
sides.
Courtesy R. Ellis

The Rotunda - 9

her eyesight completely for the rest of her life.

Children got their weekly wash and scrubbing on late Saturday afternoons, together with pocket money, to be ready for confession and to look their best on Sunday mornings. It was the time of the British colonial pounds, shillings, and pence.(A popular saying then, was: *Ħobż* = bread; *ġobon* = cheese; Malta u Għawdex *tal-Ingliż*=Malta and Gozo belong to the British).

Clergy were venerated. They were second only to our parents in order of prestige. Children were naturally deferent enough to and awed by the mere glimpse or flicker of any fluttering soutane in the street.

The two most popular barbers, *Majruzz*, and *Ganajx*, were always kept very busy cropping our heads for a sixpence. A queue was a must.

Gas cylinders were inexistent and cooking, therefore, was mainly done using kerosene stoves or dry stalks *ħatab* in a *kenur*, a stove, made of stone and kept alight using a fan *rewwieħa*.

At least three hawkers regularly supplied kerosene every week: Frenċ *taż-Żembil*, Ġanni *ta' Ċula* and Salvu *ta' Paċikk*. They each had a 55 gallon Shell or Esso metal drum, tied on a wooden cart, pulled by one of their respective docile animals.

Later on, the only television set (black and white screen, of course) that arrived in San Bert Street belonged to Ġużepp Spiteri *tal-Majru*, owner of one of the village bars.

Ġużepp, an amiable and jovial character, ran a family grocery during the day and a popular wine bar in the evening. His watering hole was intimate and a microcosm of local life, an extension of one's living room.

Children (and these meant strictly boys only) would flutter to the wine bar, like moths towards the light. It was before and after our evening religious lessons (*il-Mużew tad-Dutrina*), to buy sweets or a chocolate wagon wheel.

We would catch up wild-eyed on episodes of Gunsmoke, Lassie, Bonanza, Rin Tin Tin, Zorro and Sergente Garcia.

Alternatively, our eyes were glued to one of the many westerns with cowboys always chasing or shooting American Indians with wild abandon.

Inside the wine bar itself, a handful of crusty men held court, putting the world to rights or otherwise playing a mean game of *brixkla*. It is a card game for two or four; three cards being dealt to each player and one turned up, known as the *brixkla*.

They dealt cards around a square wooden table with a red Formica top. A pint or two of local wine the color of ripe Comino plum and a closed fist of peanuts or hard white chickpeas *ċiċri*, in front of them.

Meanwhile, at the far back corner a couple of older men, coarser, and with weathered faces, would bring their meal in a cloth bundle *sorra*, duly prepared by their wives. They would have their banquet there while watching TV, downing pints of the dark-colored wine and return home pretty imbibed.

The cloth in which they brought their meal sometimes included salty tripe or a piping hot pot brimming with rabbit stew in a rich sauce. These and other such Gozitan staples calls for lots of bread slathered with olive oil.

The *sorra* naturally also served as a napkin to wipe the inedible mess left behind and to clean their flick-knives. After slurping up the food and gulping rather than sipping the wine, loud belching was de rigeur.

A freshly rolled cigarette dangled from the mouth of those playing cards. Cigarette smoke permeated the room and rose at a sharp angle from ashtrays curling towards the high ceiling, catching the fluorescent neon tube light in between.

Peanut skins and cigarette butts littered the floor. Cursing or swearing was down to a minimum. Ġużepp, the proprietor, would not tolerate it, and he would tell you so.

Whenever the game was not going according to his liking, Ġanni, a small-time fisherman, would curse the sea without fish (*ħaqq il-baħar ta' bla ħut*). However, that is the extent of how far he would go with his soubriquet.

Ġanni, a wily card player was hard to beat in a game of brixkla. With a leathery poker face, he kept count of all the points. He knew all the cards that were dealt, and more often than not, won decisive games by a single point, even when the odds were stacked high against him.

He was a marvel to unravel his strategy. He could bluff his way through a game holding nothing. If one underestimated him, chances were that one would walk away with no change left in the pocket. Invariably Ġanni and his sidekick almost always collected their trophy: a packet of 20 cigarettes of his choice, a Du Maurier, Rothmans, Flag or Bristol.

Ġużepp was a successful winemaker and supplied a good part of the island with his inexpensive, home-made wine. It was distributed in a typical clear glass gallon bottle. We spent a lot of our time and gladly left most of our pocket money at his place.

There was always a mixed crowd. The colorful, boisterous characters usually ranged from Bennardu, the street cleaner, to Ġanni, the small-time fisherman; from the full-time farmer, Żeppu to Wistin, a stone dresser. There was the odd civil servant and naturally a couple that barely existed, in between.

One undeniably unique character was Żeppu, an old bachelor, who used to come by, almost every evening, all the way from *Taħt Il-Ħorob*. He was always chewing and eating dry fava beans. For the natural consequences this brought about, he was persuaded to leave the wine bar.

During cold winter weeks, Żeppu would shed on a long, ill-fitting, black coat bought from Toni *ta'Mallia*.

One could find just about anything one wanted from *ta'Mallia*. Toni, a clever entrepreneur, bought all the British army and navy surplus, and then some more. His huge warehouse contained bric a' brac that were hard to find in street markets. Connaisseurs and dealers came from all over the islands to find that special something. They normally did.

Żeppu cut a lone, strange, dark figure, walking down the middle of the dimly lit, utterly deserted San Bert Street.

This was just after the bar closed down for the night, and all the other doors were locked and firmly barred.

San Bert is one of the longest and ruler-straight residential streets found in Gozo. With lightning and thunder striking without respite, he would continue trudging on alone, unperturbed like a pale ghost from the past.

Tall, straight as a candle, with an upturned collar, his heavy army boots stamping down, echoing in a perfect dead silence. His appearance foreboding, casting a glittering shadow in the water puddles from the drizzling rain, Żeppu would have frightened the devil himself.

He cut an amazing figure: fearless, unrelenting, and alarming in appearance. At his sight, cats would flee rapidly and stealthily climb walls while stray dogs held their breath until he passed, with tails firmly curled between their rear legs.

In real life, he was kind and gentle, a sad giant. One could read the deep furrows on his ashen white face and see the sorrow in his bloodshot eyes, of perhaps a long, lost love. Come to think of it, Żeppu would not hurt a fly.

The real ice cream was still unheard of, then. During the hot summer days, we could only suck colored ice cubes, bought for half a penny from 'Glory of England' bar, owned by the Bonnici family *tal-Kops*.

Later in the afternoon Pawlu Rapa *ta' Saminu* would come by with his pony and fill your cup with one scoop of deliciously flavored ice. It was as good as it gets.

Children would remonstrate with him to please fill up the cup some more, but he would gently explain that he is selling his ice by the scoop, and not by the size of the glass. That is a shame many would say as we only have money for just a scoop each.

At home, most families listened to Rediffusion, a cable radio system started by the British. Bedtime in winter was normally around 8 pm, after saying prayers and the rosary, without exception, of course.

Fresh milk was obtained from Ġużepp Debono *ta' Anġolina*, who, every morning, at the crack of dawn called to our doorstep with his herd of clanging sheep and goats. He supplied the rest of the households along San Bert street at three pence a cup before returning his flock back to their pens.

One would know that Ġużepp had done his round because the street would be left littered with crottels. These were similar to black-brown bullets, some soft as sponge cakes, others hard as nails.

The milk was naturally raw, warm and frothy and heavenly. For sanitary reasons, one was supposed to boil and pasteurize the milk first, but many a times we did not wait to do so and drank it directly from the milk jug.

Then Nenu Cauchi *tax-Xiber* would come along with a cart full of wonderfully baked bread, fresh from their wood –fired oven. It is no secret that *tax-Xiber* still bakes one of the best bread on the entire island.

After doing the rounds, young Nenu, who was still a student, would send his animal back to the bakery on its own so that he could attend school. The house is today known as *Il-Berġa* (Auberge), a health clinic located next to the Police Station.

The animal would oblige and duly find its way home down St. Catherine's street, then make a sharp left turn and continue towards the end of Ħamsin Street and stop at the bakery.

After the 7 am mass, which was still said in Latin, we would sprint all the way home, to grab and possess the first kerosene cooking stove, *kuċiniera tal-ftila* and make toast. In turn, this was ladled with loads of butter that quickly melted away into the nooks and crannies of the thick bread slices, against the pleas of mother.

Cups and jugs and kettles were scattered all over the kitchen. Bottled jam when available was pure luxury.

Even at that time, mom was immensely health conscious and knew very well that too much butter and margarine was not exactly healthy.

As for us, one had to be careful then, not about cholesterol, but on how to regulate the stove's flame.

Otherwise, one was apt to blacken the whole kitchen in no time. And that would be a real chore.

An average post-war family counted some eight siblings. Most children had to make do with one pair of shoes all year round.

When these shoes became sodden, particularly during wet, cold winters, many of us ended up with open-mouth shoes, or worse, barefooted. We had to walk on cobblestones, and hard asphalt riddled with potholes, for the rest of the year, which usually meant until the feast of the Baptist. (Nike or Addidas had not made their debut yet.)

In summer this did not matter so much since hardly anyone wore shoes; so we wore them primarily to attend school and on special occasions. School uniforms were a rarity while absenteeism, truancy, and early school leaving, rampant.

It was no secret that a very limited number of students made it to either Technical School or the Lyceum in Rabat. Education, although compulsory, was still lacking and way behind in our primitive village. If it had not been for our strict, disciplinarian headmaster, Mr. Joseph J. Vella who administered without fear or favor, even the few students who graduated successfully would not have done so.

When for some reason our teacher failed to show up, Mr. Vella would come to teach us himself. If his schedule did not permit, the headmaster would fill out the entire blackboard with mathematical sums so as to keep us occupied and not waste our time idling around.

Joseph J. Vella's love for the village of Xewkija is manifested in his most beautiful anthem dedicated to the patron St. John the Baptist. This glorious anthem is known by heart by every true *Xewki* and has been passionately played and proudly sung on the *Prekursor's* feast every year without fail for the past half century.

Lunch consisted primarily of a couple of pieces of bread soaked in olive oil, tomato paste, capers and occasionally a slice of ham so thin that one could see the sun through it.

Friday's was a nugget of tuna, anchovy, and sardine or a cheese sandwich: meat was strictly prohibited. During the month of April, classrooms turned into a virtual gas chamber with everybody farting away after eating bread ladled with preserved tomato paste and loads of fava beans. The teachers joined in as well.

Those families who owned flocks of goats and sheep made delicious fresh cheeselets used in fava bean pies and tarts that one could die for. The tart included cheeselets, eggs, fava beans, peas and clumps of sweet raisins.

Soft drinks, except for a local soda called Kicks, were expensive. Only the privileged or the very well-off could afford to buy a case of Pepsi. For some reason, Coca-Cola had not yet penetrated the market in Gozo.

At school, we were all allowed a free glass of government subsidized milk every morning. Spinster Żeża or saintly Dwardu Xuereb *ta' Fittet*, rigorously supervised us. They were two of the most dedicated and reliable caretakers' one could wish.

Between them, they kept the whole school complex sparkling clean throughout the scholastic year. Some of us used to bring a tiny bottle of essence to dilute the milk and give it a taste of strawberry, banana or cherry. It was delightful.

Misbehaving was punished by getting spanked hard on your hand with a special wooden ruler. Certainly this did not happen on the watch of our kind-hearted and understanding teacher, Mr. Meilak.

Instead, he would feign as if he was going to slap one hard. However, only then Mr. Meilak would just touch your hand with the tip of the ruler and thus knighting one into the mischievous students' club. How true it is that one cannot forget a good teacher.

A couple of times during the year we had a supplement of bitter fish oil capsules to boost our omega vitamins and protein. In fact, a couple of students had shown white skin spots on their faces.

Fears were allayed, however because if found with nits one could only return to school when one was completely cured as well as against a medical certificate since head lice are highly contagious.

The month of June was naturally considered as the month of joy. It was a time when children were pregnant with high expectations of the upcoming celebration of the Feast of the Baptist. Petards lit at the crack of noon to herald the feast, resounded loudly across the island on our way home from school.

The ongoing lively decoration of the village streets contributed immensely to this joyful atmosphere. Poles, flags, and banners, statues of saints standing high on pedestals or plinths were everywhere.

This state of happiness was also because the half-day school was almost out and the sea being now relatively warm, was beckoning for a swim.

June has the longest daylight hours of the year in the Northern Hemisphere. The sun rises at 5.45 in the morning and goes down well after 8 in the evening. The summer solstice occurs on dates varying from 20th to 21st June.

Apricots, cherries, and strawberries, plums and peaches were all appetizing, but the mouth-watering fat ripe fig *bajtra ta' San Ġwann* was the most inviting and eaten in the midday summer sun.

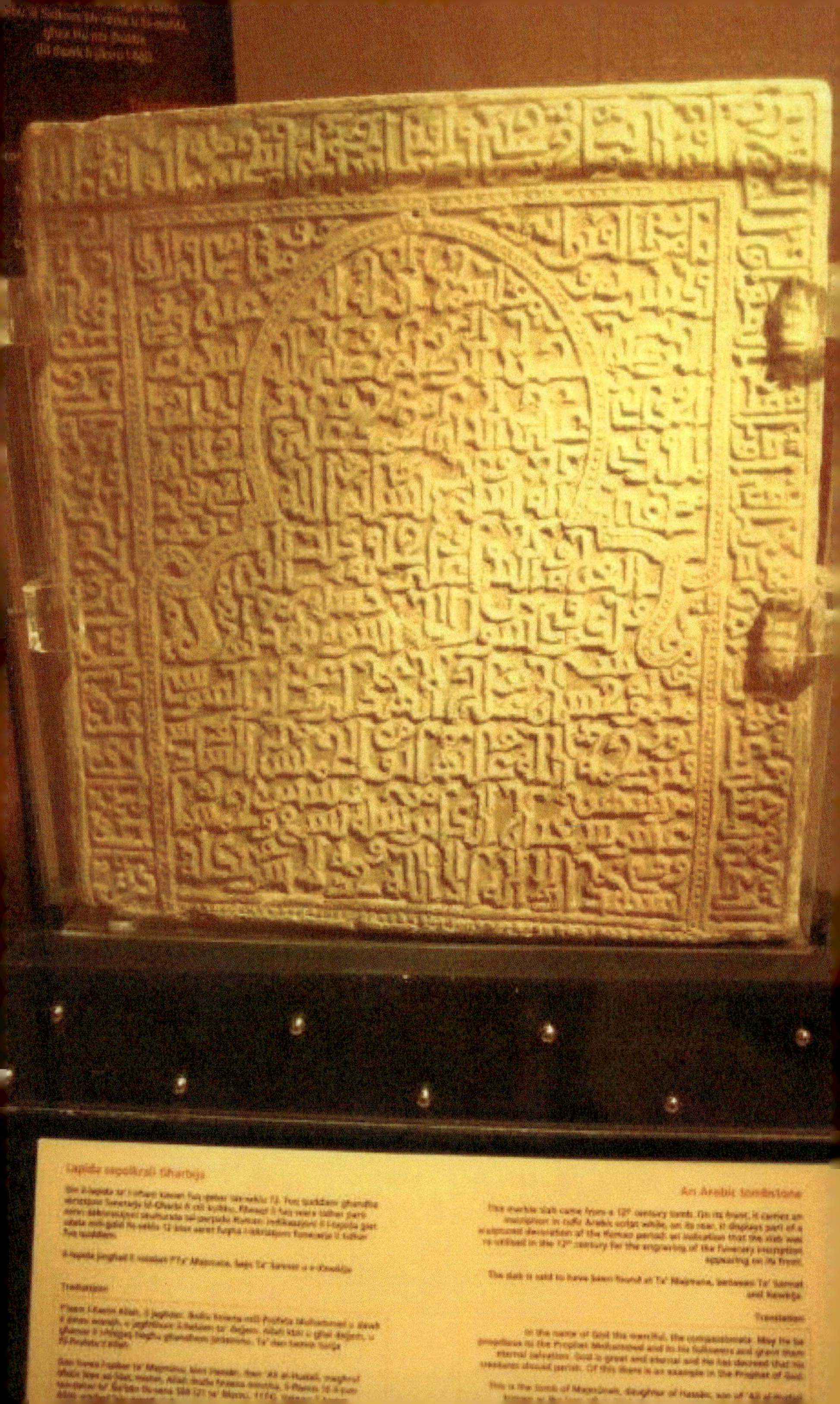
An Arabic tombstone
Translation

Chapter Two

From Paganism to Christianity

"Once we had come safely through, we discovered that the island was called Malta. The inhabitants treated us with unusual kindness. They made us all welcome."
                                    Acts of the Apostles, 28, 1-2

"And in soft meadows on either side, iris and wild celery flourished. It was indeed a spot where even an immortal visitor must pause to gaze in wonder and delight."
                                    The Odyssey, V. 74, Bk. 5 Homer

The village of Xewkija stretches from a lush plateau of *ta'l-Eħbiel* and *ta' Kotkot* to the dry crags of *Għar ix-Xiħ*. It overlooks the picturesque shingle beach of Mġarr ix-Xini and runs from *Santa Ċeċilia/ Ta' Maċedonia* Tower up to *Ġnien is-Sultan* and *Ġnien tal-Lewż*.

It covers an area of approximately 2 kilometers (1.3 square miles). At the very site of the Rotunda, it is 104 meters (341 feet) above sea level. At one time, it boasted five coastal towers.

One of these, *ta' Mastru Xmun/ ta' Ċirpisin* Tower, now also known as tal-Kosta or Santa Teodora. The tower bears an engraved stone sundial dating back to 10 April 1546, making it the oldest vertical sundial in the Maltese islands.

As one can deduce, in olden days religion was an important and major circumstance. It is exhibited by the impressive remains of pagan temples that flourished and which remains, are now scattered across the entire Maltese Archipelago.

The mysterious Maimuna Stone as displayed at the National Museum in Rabat, Gozo
Courtesy National Museum

They range from a Semitic people: the Phoenicians and the Carthaginians who worshiped their gods of Melkart and Astarte, leading to the veneration of Roman ones, such as Venere, Diana, Apollo, and Guno.

In the Acts of the Apostles, 28, 1-2, we find that St. Paul was shipwrecked on our shores. Tradition states that the first Gozitans heard St. Paul preaching from Mdina, less than 20 kilometers away while they were gathered on the high ground of the megalithic temple *Maqgħad ix-Xiħ*.

Today a marble plaque inscription in Latin which records this tradition is found in the Museum of Sculpture:

AUDIERUNT - CREDIDERUNT – CUSTODIERUNT

It praises the Xewkin for having heard, believed and safeguarded St. Paul's teaching.

An inscription in Maltese is today found upon a plinth with the statue of St. Paul, which stands outside the Rotunda, beneath the bell-tower.

There is also mention of this extraordinary event in Mdina. It says that " *li t-tromba mqaddsa ta' San Pawl semmgħet bin-noti tagħħa tas-sema lill-Għawdxin fil-Ġzira tagħħom.*" Loosely translated: "The blessed trumpet of St. Paul (the powerful voice that carries far) with its heavenly notes was heard by the Gozitans in their island."

Up until 1953, next to the old church stood a chapel dedicated to St. Paul to mark this traditional event. This chapel was eventually brought down to make way for the Rotunda.

How one could have heard, the powerful voice of St. Paul from Mdina, across the Gozo channel to Xewkija, surely beggars belief.

The following is not strictly relevant, but it is, one would think, revealing.

During the Second World War, several inhabitants of the hamlet of Għasri, particularly those with acute hearing could make out the roar of the BMW twin- engine Junkers 88. It happened just before take-off from their airfield in Comiso, Sicily. Comiso is a good distance of around 104 kilometers.

Għasri is situated at the north-westernmost part of the island. The roar could be heard during the dead of night and in prevailing winds, when the *Schnellbomber*, a high-speed bomber with a payload of 2,200 lbs., bombs was taking off.

One of these inhabitants, who could audibly hear the bewildering roar of these night-bombers as they hit maximum speed on the runway, was *iz-Zombla*, Police Constable 353 Anthony Mizzi, the writer's father.

PC Mizzi, who was stationed in this tiny village, would immediately telephone Headquarters in Malta, thereby alerting Royal Air Force (R.A.F.) command and inform them that the Luftwaffe was on its way.

At first R.A.F. could not believe him. Many thought that it must be a crank call. Besides there was no blip or any indication on the radar at Dingli Cliffs of any Junkers or Messerschmitt's, whatsoever.

However, sure enough, as the heavily loaded bombers gained altitude, R.A.F. command would confirm that, unfortunately, the deadly Junkers were by now picked up on radar heading towards Valletta and the Three Cities.

These few precious minutes gained by this timely warning let our Spitfires to scramble aloft and gave them a high angle of the climb to intercept the German bombers head on.

Meanwhile, ground artillerymen prepared their Bofors for an intermittent and deafening hack.

There is little doubt that in the process, this invaluable warning or intelligence tipoff, call it what one may, must have saved tons of war materiel and many a precious life.

In 1942, one must bear in mind that Malta was one of the most intensely and heavily bombed countries during the Second World War. The Three Cities were practically leveled to the ground. Many of the inhabitants fled to other safer villages, including Gozo.

Even the remote shrine, the majestic Basilica of Ta' Pinu was not spared. This national shrine had about 46 stained glass windows smashed by the blast of the bombs dropped by these Messerschmitt's in the vicinity of this sanctuary.

```
        D.           O.           M.
IN HONOREM S. JOHANNIS BAPTISTAE, CHRISTI PRAECURSORIS
          SANCTUM HOCCE TEMPLUM,
A MAJORIBUS HUJUS PAGI SCEUKIAE INCOLIS AEDIFICATUM
                  QUI
   D. PAULUM APOSTOLUM MELITAM APPULSUM,
        CHRISTI LEGEM CONCIONANTEM
                  HEIC
      AUDIERUNT, CREDIDERUNT, CUSTODIERUNT,
                 QUOD
   ILL. AC REV. D. FR. D. PAULUS ALPHERAN DE BUSSAN,
ARCHIEPIS. DAMIATAE INSULARUM MELITAE GAULOSQ. EPISCO
TU SOLEMNI OLEO SACRO DELINIVIT AN. Æ.V. MDCCLV. DIE XII. OC
UJUS MEMORIA IN POSTERUM DOM. III. CUJUSLIBET MENS. OCTO
              CELEBRARI DECREVIT
      POSTULANTE D. PETRO AQUILINA PAROCO P. Q. S.
```

This brings us back to the mighty voice of the Apostle Paul. During his three-month sojourn, intrepid Saul of Tarsus, although a Roman prisoner, must have stood on the high ground of the Grotto, in Rabat, outside Mdina. Here he preached the Gospel of Jesus Christ, with such force and candor, splitting the still of the late evening when nature goes to rest.

A pleasant south-easterly breeze must surely have carried his unwavering, powerful voice to those Gozitans gathered on the elevated area of *Maqgħad ix-Xiħ*, where the Rotunda presently stands.

The Maltese believed his Christian theological doctrine found in his epistles. Their faith was deep and unwavering and proudly declared 10th February, the day of his shipwreck, a Public Holiday.

St. Paul invariably became Patron of the Maltese Islands (*Missierna l-Maltin*) and remains a fountainhead of Christian Malta. Similarly, devotion to St. Paul has inevitably and markedly risen. God was now the very hub of their existence.

Another marble slab, this time a Saracenic tombstone with an engraved epitaph of a young Muslim Berber girl,

The original marble plaque which records this tradition displayed in the Museum of Sculpture.

called Majmuna, who died on March 21, 1174, echoes the Aghlabid Arab rule over the islands.

This splendid tombstone, similar to those used in Roman times, is said to have been found in the vicinity of *Ġnien is-Sultan*. It is considered to be an ancient remnant of great importance during the Arab rule of some 220 years.

Moreover, it casts a spell as it is the only one written in primitive Kufic (Arabic) characters and with such details that were ever found on the Maltese islands thus far.

There is still much mystery surrounding this magnificent stone relic, which is on display at the Museum of Archaeology in Gozo.

The inscription in Kufic calligraphy, movingly laments the death of a young girl, daughter of Hassan, son of *Ali al Hudali*, called then *as-Susi*, with these words:

> *Ask thyself if there is anything everlasting, anything that can repel or cast a spell upon death.*
> *Alas, death has robbed me of my short life; neither my piety nor my modesty could save me from him. I was industrious in my work, and all that I did is reckoned and remains. Oh, thou covered my eyelids and the corners of my eyes.*
>
> *On my couch and in my abode there is naught but tears; and (what will happen) when my Creator comes to me?*

A solid silver ring is the only other significant ornamentation found during the excavation of the Islamic cemetery with the Kufic inscription that reads: '*Rabbi Allah Wahid*' – 'God alone is the Lord'. It is today preserved at the Domvs Romana in Rabat, Malta.

Joe Zammit Ciantar, Senior Lecturer at the University of Malta, writes that,

> *"One very particular characteristic of the inhabitants of this village is that many do not pronounce the 'q' glottal stop of modern Maltese. Instead, for this consonant they used to – and some still do today – utter the ق /qaf/ of Classical Arabic. This*

may be a linguistic remnant of the Arabs' rule over the islands between 870 and 1091 A.D. Although, after the Norman Conquest the Arabs who did not convert to Christianity were expelled in 1249, those who stayed were perhaps in a great number in Xewkija. Whatever the case, this phenomenon lingers on, and people brought up in this village grow up pronouncing the ش phoneme as part of their Maltese phonetic sounds."

Interestingly, this phonetic sound is found in the ancient Aramaic alphabet that is adapted from the Phoenician alphabet. The letters all represent consonants, some of which are *matres lectionis*, which also indicate long vowels.

Therefore, from the holy Gospel according to Mark (5:21-43), one finds that Jesus said, "*Talitha, koum*," which means, "Little girl, get up."

Meanwhile, Mgr. Joseph Bezzina, Head of Department of Church History at the University of Malta, states that,

"The roots of the Maltese language were laid by these Arab-speaking Muslims, who gave the name of Għawdex to the island of Gozo and that of Mdina to the Gozo Citadel. The toponym Xewkija must have originated soon afterwards."

Chapter Three

The First Village Parish

"Hear my voice, the goodness of Can. Adrian Gourgion, Vicar General, who forked out the money for me to be produced and to sing love to my fellow people."
The inscription is on the middle bell.

"The aim of art is to represent not the outward appearance of things, but their inward significance."
Aristotle

After being evangelized by St. Paul, one could find several small chapels scattered throughout the village of Xewkija. The first chapel dedicated to St. John the Baptist, in Xewkija, is recorded in an important manuscript at the Archdiocese Malta Archives.

During the Ecclesiastical Period of Martin Rojas de Portalrubio (11/05/1572 - 03/19/1577), Monsignor Pietru Dusina established the feast of St. John the Baptist, among other feasts, as a holy day of obligation. This pastoral visit took place in 1575.

The late Emeritus Professor Godfrey Wettinger, a recognized authority on the medieval history of the Maltese Islands, writes that in 1573, Xewkija is named as a *"contrada"*, that is a suburb. Once again, this is mentioned in the year 1608 when Bishop Tomas Gargall paid a visit to this chapel.

Meanwhile, the farmsteads continued to grow and multiply. The construction of coastal fortifications made the local inhabitants more safe and secure. The marauding Turks and Berber pirates had made the sheltered inlet of Mġarr ix-Xini, literally meaning galley port, their favorite landing place in Gozo.

As a means of protection, most of the inhabitants including fishermen, lived inland for their own and their families' safety, from the fearsome Turkish Sinan Pasha.

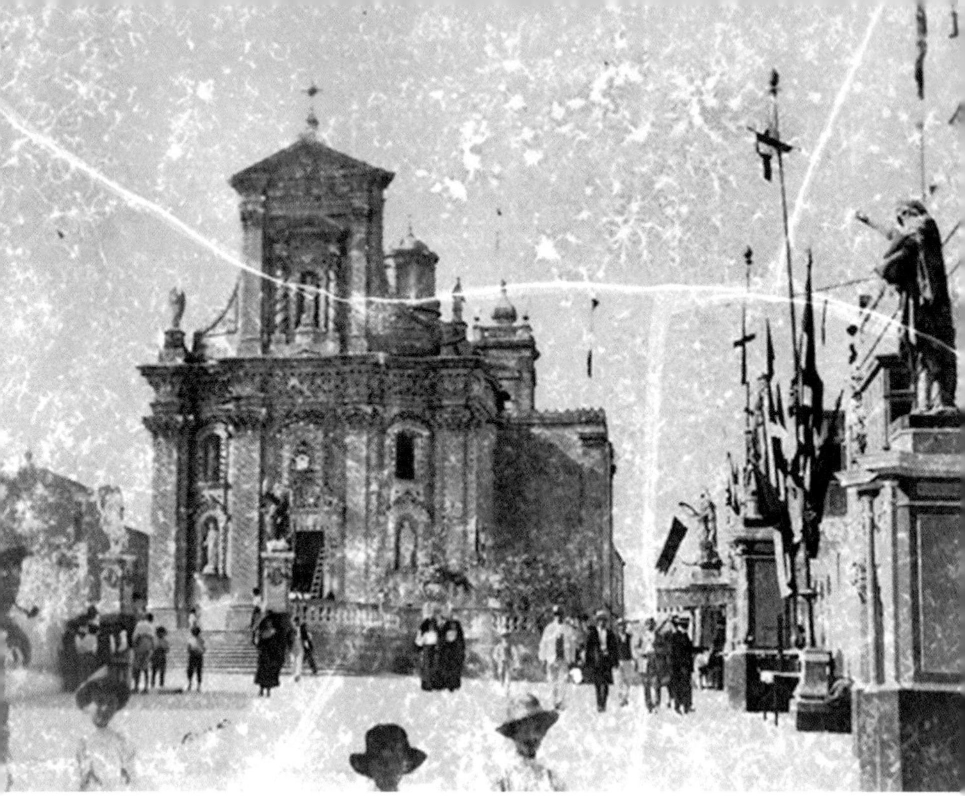

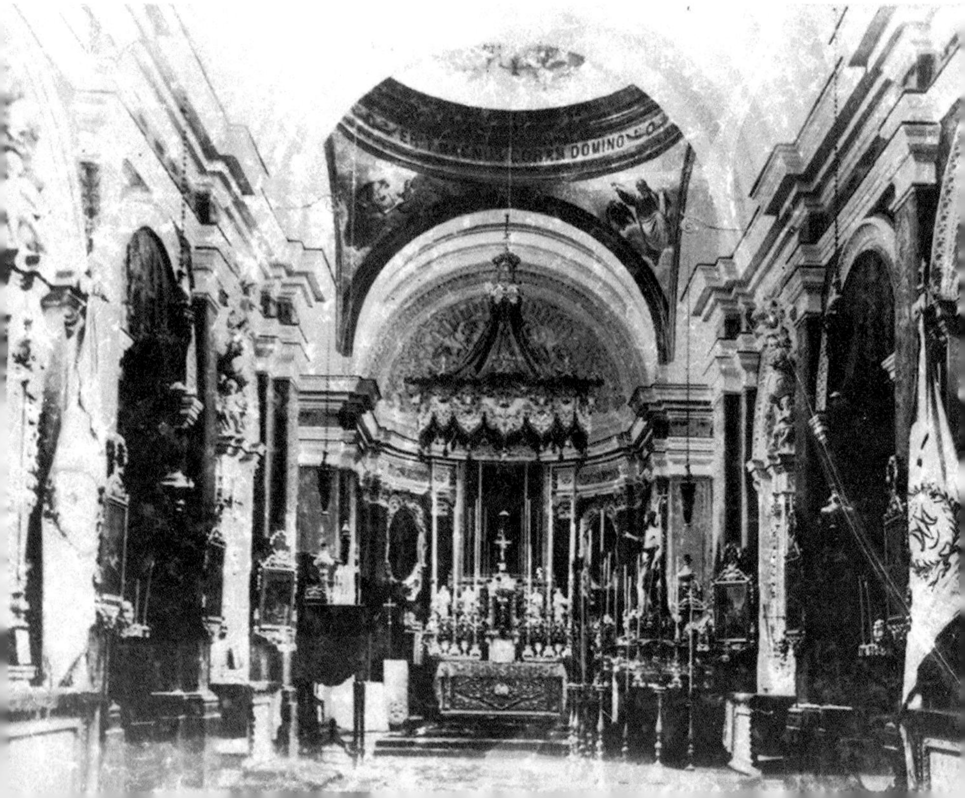
DOMINO

Up until April of 1637, Gozitans were ordered to spend the night in the Citadel stronghold. When the law was repealed, many residents spread and settled in the surrounding countryside.

Historical records indicate that the fastest growing area in Gozo was Xewkija. A delightful warren of medieval streets and alleys and squares and passageways began to develop rapidly into a village.

The inhabitants of Xewkija presented a petition to Bishop Michele de Molina. They respectfully requested an autonomous parish from the Matrice parish within the Citadel in Rabat so that these 646 inhabitants would not have to travel a considerable distance to fulfill their spiritual obligations.

Bishop Molina felt that their request was justified. So on 27 November 1678, the last day of his pastoral visit to the island, Bishop Molina, issued a decree establishing Xewkija as the first parish in Gozo. Dun Grezz Farrugia from Valletta, became the first parish priest.

Half a century later, on the initiative of the hard-working parish priest, Dun Dumink Abela (1694 -1734) a bigger church was erected on the same site of the original chapel. Dun Dumink succeeded notwithstanding a multitude of difficult conditions.

It was built by Gozitan chief mason Ferdinand Valletta. The church was planned and designed in the form of a Latin cross on a north-south axis by Ġużepp Azzopardi from Birgu, Malta.

Archpriest Cassia Magri from the Matrice of the Gozo Cathedral solemnly blessed the church on 17 March 1728. The apse behind the high altar and those in the transepts carved in the soft limestone "lace" sculpture of 1665 were incorporated into this church.

This magnificent ornate Baroque façade is probably to be the work of two Sicilian refugees, who like Caravaggio, escaped from their country after committing a crime or running afoul of the law. These Sicilians sought refuge in the village of Xewkija.

The incredibly fine sculpture better known as Rococo

depicts an array of droves of seraphim angels, puttini as described in the Apocalypse of St. John in the Book of Revelation. These guardians of the heavens give it a most heavenly character. Moreover, the intricate carving and the delicate finish have been rightly judged a masterpiece. Mario Fenech, a historian, points out that this outstanding piece of workmanship is very similar to that found in the Co-Cathedral of St. John in Valletta.

The only difference between the two is in the middle scene of the apse. One bears the image of the Holy Spirit in the form of a Dove while the one found at Xewkija depicts the Lamb of God.

The connection of the Order of the Knights of St. John with the village of Xewkija is strong. The Order ruled supreme in our islands for well over 250 years. Its crusading knights, "the flower of European aristocracy", left part of a mysterious and enchanting heritage of Baroque churches and cathedrals whose walls are still adorned with the work of famous artists. These include Caravaggio, Antoine de Favray, Mattia Preti and Gioacchino Loretta.

Part of the spoils from the Battle of Lepanto included chalices, incense burners with solid candlesticks, silver lamps, and other precious silverware.

The titular painting of St. John the Baptist in the wilderness', a gift of Bishop Molina, is attributed to Gioacchino Loretta, (circa 1637-1712), who hailed from the school of Mattia Preti.

According to Paul Falzon, a history academic who has written a scholarly thesis on the artist, Loretta based this painting on the chiaroscuro of Caravaggio. It is, Falzon continues, one of the best Baroque paintings of the 17th century.

Joe Camilleri, probably the most authoritative art critic on our island for the past half century, writes that this painting reminds one of the figures painted on the ceiling of the Co-Cathedral of St. John.

Camilleri points out that the Caravaggesque chiaroscuro is the work of a skilled master and concludes that this titular painting is one of the best artistic works that are to be found in Gozo.

Similarly the titular painting that is above the high altar in the Augustinian church in Rabat portraying St. Augustine with St. John the Baptist and St. William of Aquitaine, is attributed to Mattia Preti.

The similarity of both these titular paintings is intrinsic if not intriguing. St. Augustine was commissioned and paid for by Giovanni Gourgion.

Meanwhile, Mario Fenech concludes that since their arrival in Malta, the Knights set their eyes on the village of Xewkija by commissioning and donating several precious works.

The parish church of Xewkija was consecrated by Bishop Fra Pawlu Alpheran de Bussan on 12th October 1755. The church was constructed on the design of a cross with Doric columns. The round roof boasted curved structural moldings that formed an intricate framework.

A couple of decades later, in 1774, another resourceful parish priest, Dun Franġisk Mizzi, added a bell tower.

Canon Adrian Gourgion, who was Vicar General generously, donated the middle bell (*Fustanija*) with a most eloquent inscription in Latin that read:

> "*Vox Adriani Gourgion, Can. Cath. et V.G. munificentiam sonat, incolarum canit amorem.*" -- "hear my voice, the goodness of Can. Adrian Gourgion, Vicar General, who forked out the money for me to be produced and to sing love to my fellow people."

Canon Adrian came from an illustrious family, probably the noblest family that ever lived in Xewkija. His brother, Giovanni Gourgion, a Knight of Saint John of Jerusalem, was private secretary to Grand Master Fra' Adrien de Wignacourt.

He used to spend his holidays together with other knights at their sumptuous Gourgion castle that was built in 1688.

It was located a short distance to the south of the parish church, amidst meadows and large terraced fields far and wide, over the beautiful valley of Mġarr ix-Xini. From here Malta's coast across the channel is clearly visible.

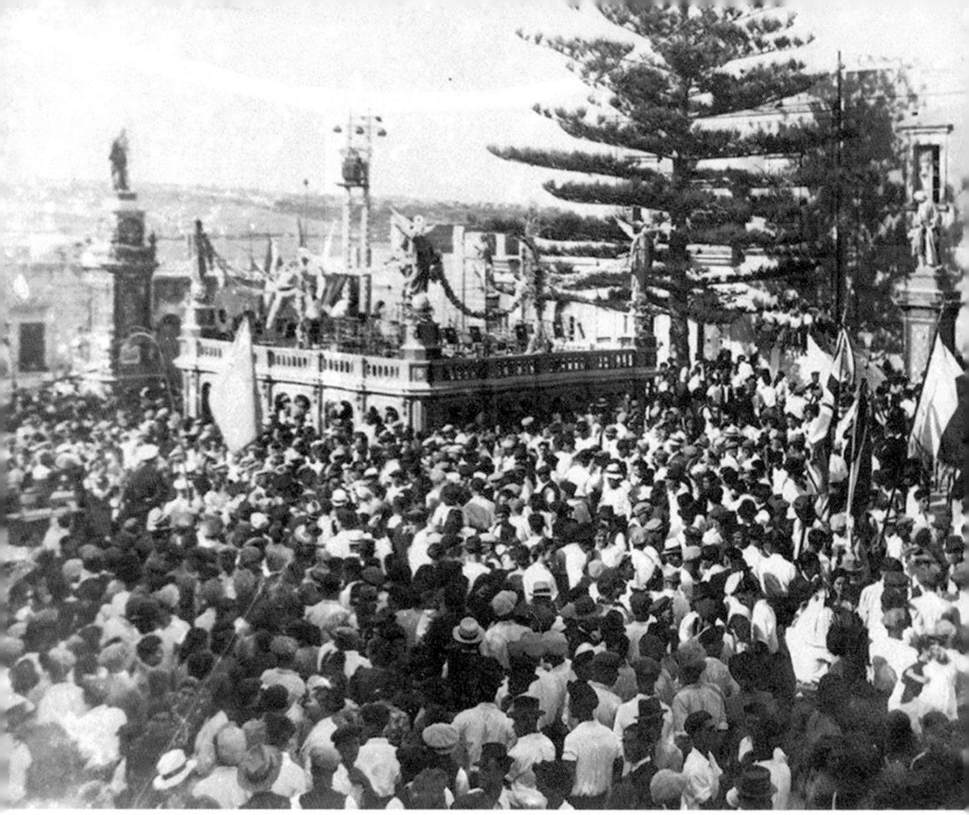

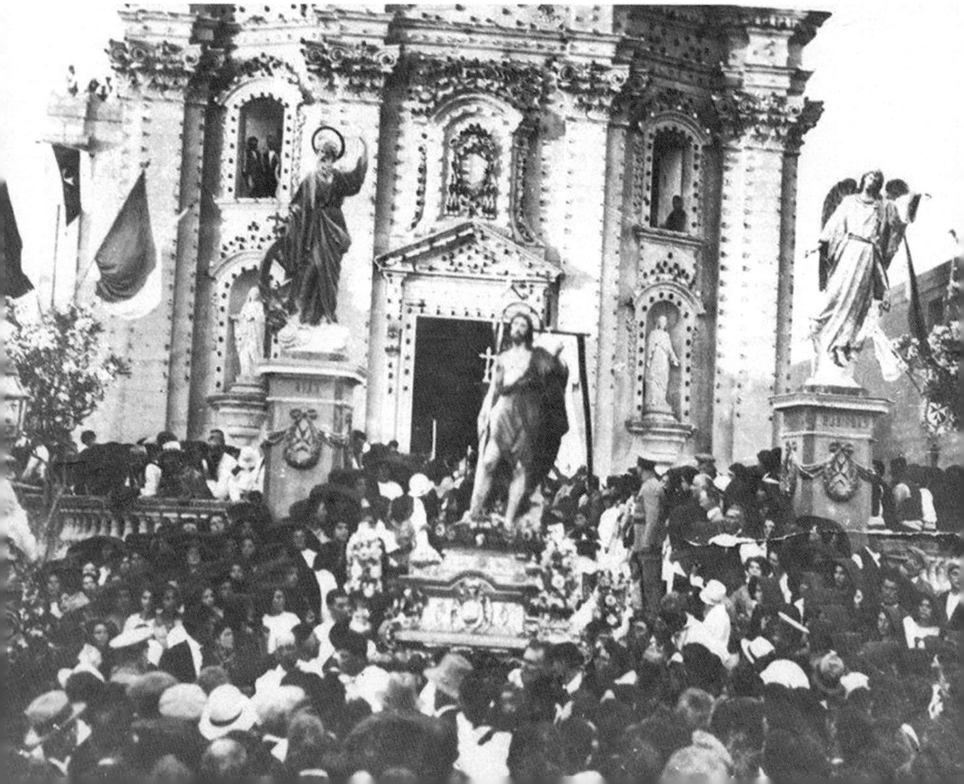

During hot summer days, the writer would descend a height of some two storeys down an extremely steep rock cliff at the back of our garden on San Bert Street. This dirt road is certainly not for the drunk or fainthearted. Many used this road as a shortcut to Mġarr ix-Xini.

The writer remembers when, together with my elder brother Ġanni, and his friend Franġisku (Frans) Azzopardi *tal-Bokki*, we stepped precariously barefoot over the freshly harvested wheat fields. It has a brownish hue that unbelievably pricked like wild thorns.

Once down in the *wilġa*, we walked past over parched soil where this landmark tower once stood until we reached a dirt road that eventually led to a footpath. We climbed down the steps hewn out of the sheer rock cliffs and went for a swim at *il-Port*, as it is still colloquially referred to by most locals.

Il-Port, is a kind of a small fjord, an inlet with a dazzling of colorful hues bursting like an abstract painting. It boasts emerald green waters, clear waters that are cobalt blue, azure waters, waters so calm that often its surface reflects like glass.

It is ideal to jump from the rock cliffs, into these warm, inviting waters. Easy to swim across to the other side of the creek, dive for sea urchins, *rizzi* or pluck out small clams and other tasty shellfish like a baby octopus. However, nothing beats the sweet and briny orange of the sea urchin. In mid-August numerous children leap in and out of the water like a group of aquatic penguins.

Every time thoughts come about our summer jaunts to *il-Port*, the writer can still feel the sharp sting on the soles of his tender feet, particularly when we stepped on the sturdy dry stalks. These were cut down with a hand sharp sickle during harvest time.

It is small wonder that Angelina Jolie and her hubby Brad Pitt chose this picturesque shingle beach to shoot their movie, 'By the Sea'.

Tamara Hinson of CNN has recently named Mġarr ix-Xini as one of 10 places in the world which should be visited before they change forever.

The main square full of people from all over the island listening to the *Prekursur* Band.

The feast of St. John the Baptist of yesteryear. Women weaing the traditional *Għonnella*, a rustic headgear of a village woman, now out of use.

The 170 years old statue of the Patron St. John the Baptist by Pietro Paolo Azzopardi (1845).

One of the columns in the courtyard of this fortified Gourgion tower had an inscription to mark the event when the *Xewkin* heard St. Paul preaching from Malta. They thus became the very first Christians in Gozo.

Sadly, this unique 17th-century tower that was an architectural gem with a style of its own was demolished. It was razed to the ground in 1943 by the American Seabees (construction battalions), to make way for a temporary airstrip for the invasion of Sicily. It was abandoned a month or so after that.

A great patriot managed with a broken heart to collect and salvage all the escutcheons, carved inscriptions, and several other sculpted stones from this glorious heritage. This was none other than Chevalier Lorenzo Zammit Haber *ta' Lawrenzu*. A commemorative postage stamp would not be amiss to this "quintessential antiquarian".

Fr. Geoffrey Attard writes that "*Zammit Haber was chosen by the British Governor in Malta to take Major*

Hugh Braun's place as an esteemed member of the Ancient Monuments Committee."

These remnants are all that is left for posterity can now be found at the Museum of Archaeology at the Citadel, Rabat. A large deep cistern in the main courtyard of the tower had a skull overhead that served to remember the dead but also to remind the living that we, too, will die. This well was annihilated and filled with the same rubble from the destruction of this tower during the construction of the said runway.

The cistern used to serve as a temporary respite, particularly for those pilgrims who were on their way to visit the Sanctuary of Our Lady of Conception in Qala.

From 1803 to 1850 Dun Nikol Vella, from Għarb became the fourth parish priest. During his 47 years in office, precisely in 1830 the dome was raised, that is, after 102 years since the church was first built.

Seven years later the chapel of St. Teodora was built to hold the martyr's mortal remains brought from Rome to Xewkija in 1836. Later this became known as the chapel of the Blessed Virgin Mary of Sorrows.

Why did the village of Xewkija choose the Baptist and why did this prophet mean so much to the villagers? Perhaps the following by Alban Goodier, S.J., can shed more light:

"Can we now picture to ourselves this first appearance of the Baptist? He came and stood in the desert by the river, at the gateway leading into Judea, on the very spot that was still hallowed by the memory of the Prophet Elias, hard upon the main road along which the busy world had to pass; a weird, uncouth, unkempt, terrible figure, in harmony with his surroundings, of single mind, unflinching, fearing none, a respecter of no person, asking for nothing, to who the world with its judgments was of no account whatever though he showed that he knew it through and through, all its castes and all its colors. He came the censor of men, the terror of men, the warning to men, yet winning men by his utter sincerity; telling them plainly the truth about themselves and forcing them to own that he was right; drawing them by no soft inducements, but by the hard lash of his words, and by the solemn threat of doom that awaited them who would

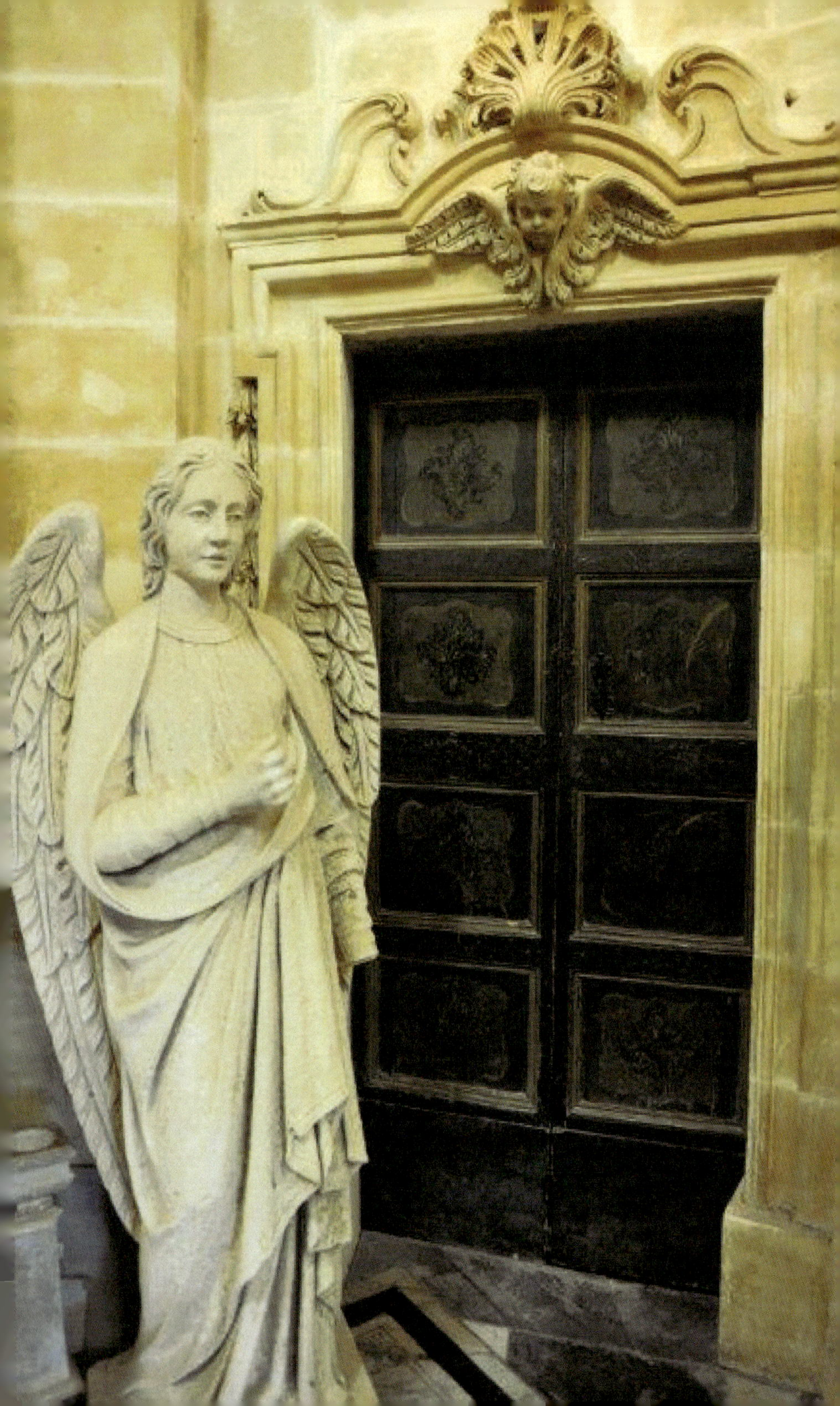

not hear; distinguishing true heart-conversion from the false conversion of conformity, religion that lived in the soul from that sham thing of mere inheritance and law. John, the focus upon which all the gathered light of the Old Dispensation converged, from which was to radiate the light of the New."

On 22nd June 1845 the titular statue of St. John the Baptist was blessed amidst joy and celebration of the people of Xewkija. This striking statue, greatly inspired by Gioacchino Loretta's St. John the Baptist in the Wilderness, is a veritable masterpiece.

It was sculpted from the main trunk of a mulberry tree by the renowned sculptor Pietro Paolo Azzopardi (1791-1875) from Valletta.

Dun Ġwann Grech *ta' Marjanu*, goes on to state that this statue was greatly admired by several respected medical doctors, particularly for its magisterial human anatomy that the skilled Azzopardi so successfully expressed.

This biblical prophet transmits with high power his austere and genuine character. Dun Ġwann further maintains that in his opinion, this renders the statue of St.John the Baptist the best work that Azzopardi ever produced.

On the occasion of the 170 years of this titular statue, Paul Cassar writes that *"Azzopardi was a source of inspiration for other artists that were inspired from the artistic greatness of this statue..."*

In his book, *'Ix-Xewkija Fi Ġrajjiet Il-Kappillani u L-Arċiprieti Tagħha'*, Father Serafin Borg, O.S.A., records that, from 1850 to 1864, there were three other parish priests. These were Dun Pawl Grech from Għarb (1850-1854); Dun Demetriju Galea, also from Għarb (1854-1859); and Dun Pietru Bartolo, from Gharghur (1859-1864). The latter built the vestry of the existing church.

Dun Pietru Pawl Ciantar (1865 -1908) became the first archpriest from Xewkija. During his 42 years in tenure, a churchyard was built on the eastern side of the church.

In 1875, a huge, mechanical clock was installed on the church façade by Mikelanġ Sapiano. Today it is in the belfry tower and can be heard from almost every quarter

The original wooden door of the old church and Archangel Gabriel

of the village. A year later, in 1876 a chapel built by Mason Ġużepp Farrugia was added.

That same year, on the occasion of the visit of His Royal Highness the Price of Wales, Xewkija was presented with a coat-of-arms. It consists of a golden shield with a horizontal red bar in the middle, on the upper and lower part of which there are two thorn blossoms. *Xewk* in Maltese means 'thorn', therefore the name Xewkija. Its motto says *"Nemo Me Impune Lacessit"*, that is, "Nobody can insult me without being punished".

An exquisite baldaquin projecting above the main altar designed by Pawlu Bugeja and gilded by master Bartoli was inaugurated in 1880. Chevalier Lorenzo Zammit Haber and his family wove the splendid drapery. This canopy remains one of the oldest and most precious treasures on the island.

The population continued to increase and the second church became small once more. In 1890, an urgent need was felt to enlarge the old church but the Ecclesiastical authorities turned it down. Therefore, it was decided to lengthen the main aisle of the church, and add a new baroque façade, very much similar to that of the Gozo Cathedral.

Dun Ġuzepp Diacono designed this façade. Two side altars were added as well. These featured in the prolonged nave. On 10 February 1893, parish priest Dun Pietru Pawl Ciantar was granted the title of archpriest given directly to him by Pope Leo XIII. The Papal Bull is today found in the archives of the parish.

That same year, on 20 June, the large bell costing 400 pounds sterling and weighing well over 35 tons was blessed and installed in the belfry under the expert supervision of Ġużepp Farrugia.

This bell was founded by Giulio Cauchi of Għajn Dwieli, Bormla. Campanologist Kenneth Cauchi considers it to be one of Cauchi's best sounding bells.

Fr. Emmanuel Magri S.J., one of Malta's pioneers in archeology found part of the Neolithic temple during his trial excavations and *"a good crop of vase fragments of varnished incised pottery."* This discovery was on 21 October 1904.

In his 'First Report – Ruins of a Megalithic Temple at Xeuchia (Shewkiyah) Gozo', Magri recounts that, *"The landlord, the Very Revd. P.P. Ciantar, very kindly allowed me to carry on my exploration and to take the ordinary finds."*

Archpriest Dun Anton Aquilina (1908-1920) did his utmost to enlarge the church, but his plans met with several obstacles and eventually did not obtain the required permits.

Dun Anton Aquilina was succeeded by Dun Anton Grima, who became Archpriest on 31st October 1920. The latter was from a family of five other priests. Dun Ġwann Grech describes him with an apt English saying as, "The man who knew his job well."

On 30 December 1922 archpriest Grima made a formal request to the bishop pointing out the urgency of building bigger naves. These were approved the following year by Bishop Mikiel Gonzi.

However, works did not start until 1936 and finished two years later by local mason Mikiel Xerri *ta' Xmun*. Six side altars together with the old sculpture were relocated and rebuilt with the utmost care and the expert ability of Anġlu Haber.

Chevalier Lorenzo Zammit Haber personally and meticulously supervised all these works. Zammit Haber also drew the detailed plans for the extension of the cemetery and the building of a new chapel. This work was carried out by another local mason Salvu Xerri *tac-Ċiklipens*.

In 1929, on the initiative of Wenzu Cauchi *ta' Dun Franġisk* and under the genial direction of Maestro Andrija Borg, *tal-Menżelett* from Rabat, the Prekursur band was established.

A parish house adjacent to the church was constructed to accommodate archpriest Grima and those that followed him. Electricity was installed for the first time in the church under the supervision of Nikola Agius *tal-Penzier* from Rabat.

The year 1945 marked the first centenary of the arrival of the statue of St. John in Xewkija. To mark the occasion four bands took part in this feast: "La Valette", "Il-Banda San Ġiljan", "La Stella" and "Leone".

Pawlu Azzopardi *ta' Ħakku*, the writer's grandfather donated another statue of St. John with lamb for this memorable occasion. This statue is the work of Gozitan artist, Chevalier Wistin Camilleri. Pawlu had the biggest fishing *luzzu* in Mġarr. Besides his vessel, he also had a spouse and eleven children.

Wistin's son, Paul, an eminent artist himself, recounted to the writer how his father Wistin brought a live lamb in his studio at Għajn Qatet. This lamb served as a model when sculpting the beautiful statue.

Today, this statue of the 'little Baptist' is paraded annually, down San Bert Street every Thursday night during the third week of June, when celebrating the Feast of the Forerunner of Christ. It is accompanied by two marching bands, one of them the *Prekursur*.

The band march starts from the crossroads of the chapel of Our Lady of Mercy *tal-Ħniena*, all the way to the main square. This vastly popular march is followed by one of the largest alcohol-fuelled fun loving crowds on the island.

However, one has to be there to see and feel the atmosphere of joy and happiness. The open and warm nature of the young people accompanying this yearly event is second to none.

Emmanuel Portelli *tal-Bellusa*, and his immediate family are the current proud curators of this exquisite statue.

A year later the feast of the Birth of the Baptist was no longer to be celebrated on the 24th of June as a holy day of obligation but on the third Sunday of June.

After 26 years of service, archpriest Dun Anton Grima passed away on 20 January 1947. He was succeeded by Dun Ġuzepp Grech, also from Rabat.

A new era dawned for Xewkija.

Chapter Four

It Takes a Village (and One Shilling)

"I know that we are ready to make great sacrifices for our Protector, St. John the Baptist, because his name is sculpted in our heart, his name is honey on our lips, his name is harmony to our ears and fills our heart with joy and peace.
God sent me amongst you not to live a comfortable life or to become rich, but to strive for the Glory of God."
Archpriest Ġużeppi Grech

The heart has its reasons, of which reason knows nothing.
Blaise Pascal

From the very beginning of the 20th century, the people of Xewkija harbored the idea to build a bigger church. The village population was growing by approximately 100 persons every year, and it now numbered over 3,500 individuals.

The old church became too small to carry out proper religious services. As we have seen earlier, during the time of archpriest Dun Pietru Pawl Ciantar, the Ecclesiastical Authorities turned down his request for a new church. Instead, the main aisle and a new façade were added to the existing structure.

Then archpriest Dun Anton Grima saw the need to enlarge the church with new naves. However, this did not solve the problem either. Archpriest Grech understood the problem very well. The solution to overcoming the overcrowding, damp humidity, the low ceiling, plus lack of ventilation of the old church was one and only one: to build a bigger church.

On 9 August 1947, the archpriest and the clergy together with a committee composed of the leading villagers unanimously concluded that for the parishioners to be served well, a new church was a must. It would have to be big enough to accommodate everyone.

Archpriest
Ġuzeppi Grech.

Architect
Ġuze' D'Amato.

Two sketches of the proposed Rotunda Church designed by architect Ġuze' D'Amato

The whole village backed them. Foremost amongst them were Chevalier Lorenzo Zammit Haber, Marċell Mercieca *tal-Gardell*, Ġużeppi Xuereb *tal-Bilbel*, Żakkarija Cilia *tal-Ġerrej*, Nazzarenu and Joseph Calleja *tal-Kerewn*, Pawlu Grech *ta'Bejża*, Pietru Xuereb, Ġanni, and Ġużepp Vella.

Bishop Pace was not amused. To build a new church meant that one had to find another place where to hold service until this new structure was finished. The parishioners could not be denied their spiritual needs.

So when architect Chevalier V. Bonello presented the freshly drawn plans of the new church, these were immediately turned down. The plans were deemed unacceptable as the old church needed to stand in place while the new one was being built.

A different site was not even considered primarily for two reasons: the church did not have any land available. Secondly, if there were, this would most likely split the village with two different churches and probably sow the seeds of bitter rival factions.

In two years' time, the ambitious archpriest Grech acquired five plots of land adjacent to the old church, by donation. Five separate contracts were made, four of which were signed and sealed in front of notary Franġisk Refalo; the first contract was signed on 27th April 1949 and the last one on 14th July 1950.

Taċ-Ċiantar family donated at least two of these plots known as *Iċ-Ċens*, and the local Government freely ceded other small plots of land as well. Today the street behind the church is named in memory of the late Archpriest Pietru Pawl Ciantar.

Archpriest Grech would not budge and was determined to get his church built; he would not take no for an answer. He promptly approached Mr. Ġuze' D'Amato, an engineer and designer by profession, from Raħal Ġdid.

Born in Sfax, D'Amato was an expert in the building of concrete and was pleased and honored with this challenge. He duly obliged and drew a grandiose plan to encompass the old church.

The immense new plan was in the form of *"Croce Greca"*.

Octagonal from the outside, but under the dome itself, it formed a circle in modified Baroque, consisting of six side chapels.

The façade consists of four built-in columns rising all the way up to the frieze and the cornice. It has four niches, two on each side on top of each other with a massive door in between. A triumphal arch on top of this door crowns the main entrance. A total of twenty niches with shallow recesses, ten on each side further complements the octagonal church from the outside.

On paper, the dome was 37.5 meters (123 feet) high and 35.3 meters (116 feet) wide. The outside diameter measured 54 meters (117 feet) and that inside 35 meters (115 feet). The majestic dome was to rest on eight reinforced concrete Corinthian columns in the form of a perfect circle and rise to a dizzying height of around 75 meters (246 feet). It would have a capacity of 3,000 people sitting and another 4,000 standing.

Bishop Pace was less amused. This plan bore more than a striking resemblance to the graceful baroque church of Santa Maria della Salute, in Venice. This church is at the tip end of the Canal Grande, near the 'Dogana da mar', or 'Punta del sale', across from San Marco.

There is no question that Santa Maria della Salute is one of the most famous and beautiful churches in the world. Little wonder then, why the people of Xewkija were head over heels with joy when they saw the plans drawn by D'Amato. It was to be a gem.

There were two major differences between the two churches. D'Amato placed the cupola over the front entrance while that of the Salute was at the back, over the presbytery.

Furthermore, the Xewkija church was markedly different. The dome was planned to rest on eight Corinthian columns forming a perfect circle; that of the Salute is octagonal from the inside. When it was built, the dome of Santa Maria della Salute was an important landmark on the Venice skyline, symbolizing triumph over adversity. The church soon became emblematic of the city, inspiring artists like Canaletto, J.W.M.Turner, John Singer Sargeant and Francesco Guardi. It has featured in almost all the major films shot in Venice, including the James Bond series.

It is worth noting what the famous architect Baldassare Longhena (1598 – February 18, 1682), who was then 26 years old, wrote." I have created a church in the form of a Rotunda, a work of new invention, not built in Venice, a work very worth and desired by many...with what little talent God has bestowed upon me of building the church in the...shape of a crown."

On paper, the Xewkija Rotunda was remarkable. But how on earth, argued the bishop and his close monsignors, can the tiny village of Xewkija build a grandiose church of this magnitude? Especially when their forefathers took over a whole century to complete the little dome of their old church!

How is it possible that an impoverished village of two dozen fishermen and some fifty farmers eclipse the Doge of the immensely rich city of Venice, a major maritime power, with a bigger church, to boot?

Xewkija had no explorers to speak of, the like of Marco Polo. A distant, well-travelled seafarer at best was perhaps Orazio Mizzi *tal-Kaptan*. However, this pales into insignificance.

How can a village of 700 odd families construct a church on the same level as that built by one of the first merchant bankers of the world?

Again how can a bishop possibly be expected to grant permission when in our islands there were half-finished churches on a far smaller scale? Most likely these wonderful plans will remain forever on paper. And many a Gozitan concurred.

For this was just a dream, a pipe dream, at best, and the *Xewkin* were told so to their faces. That one simply cannot build such a grand church with 'half pennies'or '*bid-deffun*', the latter being ground pottery used as cement for roof surfaces.

This ambitious project was deemed to be way beyond what the village of Xewkija could seriously handle. These were superb plans and designs, yes, but realistic, hardly.

The bishop found himself torn between a rock and a hard place. He needed to be concretely convinced, that the construction of the church will not start and then falls by the wayside and stalls for lack of funds. The bishop demanded that first archpriest Grech should collect a substantial amount of money before he may reconsider his decision.

Another condition was *sine qua non*, coming from none other than, *Din L-Art Ħelwa*, a non-profit heritage foundation. The foundation unequivocally demanded that the priceless and outstanding 'lacework' sculpture in the old church must be saved and rebuilt in the building underneath the belfry.

It included the ornate marble iconography floor of tombstones, some of which are inscribed with text in Latin. These were onerous conditions but all extremely valid and legitimate requests that require justifiable actions, nonetheless. After all, the proof of the pudding is in the eating.

And this, contemplated archpriest Grech humbly and silently alone, many a night in his parish house, entailed supreme courage, sacrifice, and money. Yes, lots of money and hard work. You will see, he pondered when you fry the eggs.

However, there was no going back. It was time to be able to bite the bullet and to go right on. One could not have decent religious service with or without pomp in the old church. It was too small to accommodate such crowds that thronged the church.

People were practically lying on the cold tessellated marble floor slabs of those buried beneath, sitting on top of each other, particularly on the side of the altar of All Souls, gasping for air. There was no space. Many are those that can firmly attest to this harsh reality.

As was the custom at that time, several parishioners brought their chairs to church and tied them before they returned home. Those who stood behind the naves could not see or hear anything.

The church itself stunk of humidity. No matter how many branches of carob and bay trees one brought inside, the *millipede* smell was most unkind. By some fluke, they kept creeping up from underneath the tombs without respite since the church itself served for many decades as a cemetery and an ossuary.

No matter how many times they disinfected and Vera *tar-Riħ* (sister of Dun Luċjan Debono) and her helpers washed and cleaned the church every weekend, still the smell was unpleasantly pervading.

It was also unsanitary, thought archpriest Grech. God forbid if another outbreak of cholera, which left 42 people dead in Xewkija, happened again. That was in 1837. There was an ex-voto for deliverance. God, please, perish the thought.

The village of Xewkija was far from a major maritime power; it had no Doges or merchant bankers and was certainly no major center for commerce or trade. It controlled no vast sea empire nor was it extremely wealthy to compete with other empires like that of Constantinople.

Notwithstanding this, archpriest Grech carefully considered and weighed his options before deciding to address his loyal flock. Without being overbearing, Grech was brave enough to do something when one feels sufficiently convinced to be right. He transformed his fears into a vision that only a leader of his caliber could muster. It was to be his finest sermon.

It was the Sunday before the feast of St. John the Baptist of 1948 when the whole village was in festive mode. Archpriest Grech gingerly climbed the steps to the pulpit to address the faithful thus:

"The time has come to start our work. Whoever has courage, good will, and is ready for sacrifice, succeeds. I expect that every one of you will help with prayers, work, and money, so that in the shortest time possible, the wish of our fathers and ours will be fulfilled."

"I know that we are ready to make great sacrifices for our Protector, St. John the Baptist, because his name is sculpted in our heart, his name is honey on our lips, his name is harmony to our ears and fills our heart with joy and peace."

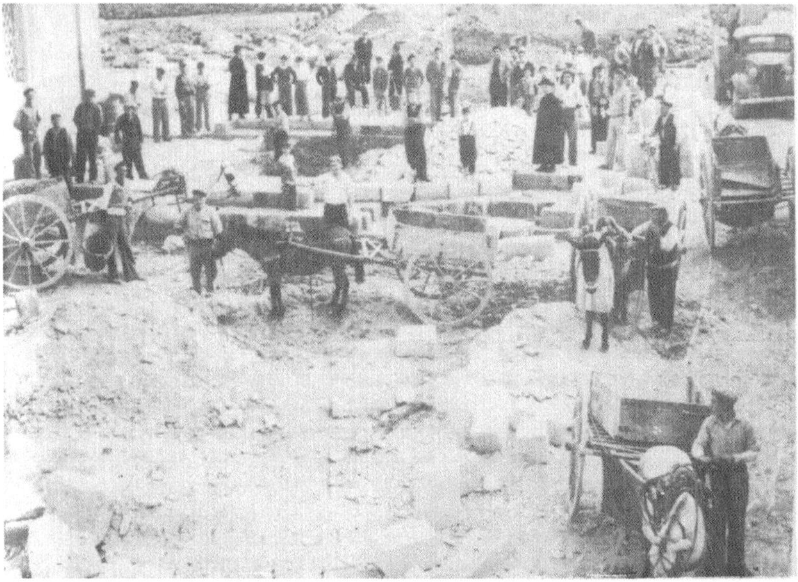

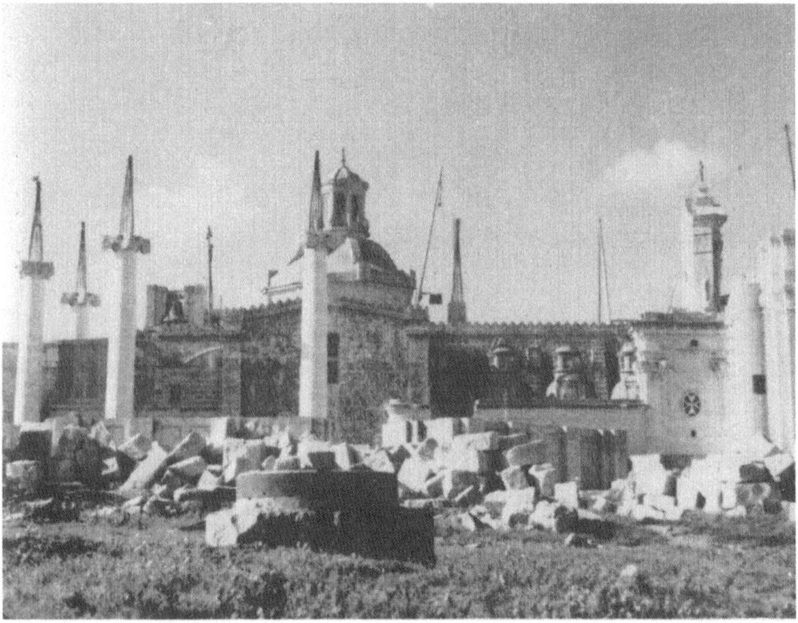

"God sent me amongst you not to live a comfortable life or to become rich, but to strive for the glory of God."

Adjusting his round, tortoise-shell spectacles, and bearing gently down on his true believers, who packed the small tight church from nave to nave, he continued, his voice unwavering,

"I promise you that I will give my health, wealth and all that I acquire, and I will die for the good and well-being of this village that is sealed with love in my heart."

Those listening were emotionally moved. Many shed a tear. They knew what he was asking, and they were determined not to let him down.

They all rose and gave him a standing ovation as he climbed down from the old wooden pulpit. Archpriest Grech had captured their imagination.

Clearing the rubble to make way for the huge foundations of the new church

The clergy also came out strongly with, *An Appeal To the People of Xewkija*. It was sent in the form of a leaflet to all the households. They asked two things. Primarily, that the church does not remain on paper but becomes a reality by starting to build it. Secondly, that when they start building the church, work will not stop until it is finished. The target date was twenty years.

The die was cast. Amidst great enthusiasm, in June of 1948, an incredible sum of 18,000 pounds sterling was collected. There was great astonishment.

A host of gold and silver items such as earrings, rings, gold chains, watches, bracelets, pendants, and even diamonds together with other jewelry were willingly donated. It amounted to almost 4,000 pounds sterling.

By all means, this was a record-breaking sum. The phenomenal spirit created by their faith in the Baptist and the generosity of the *Xewkin* was manifest. It shone as bright as the noon sun. There wasn't a single family that didn't give its share. Everyone gave until it hurt.

Six columns sprouting from the ground

This sum exceeded all proportions and superseded all calculations and expectations; it was beyond imagination and powerfully persuasive. The people spoke, and they bellowed with their pockets. There was no turning back now.

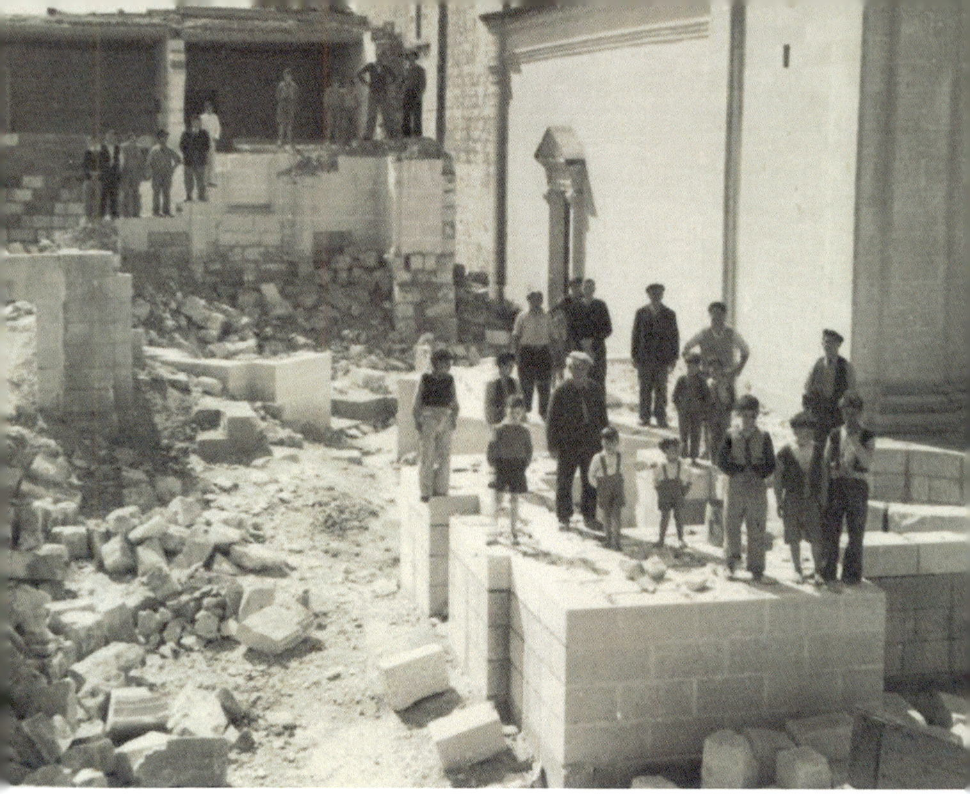

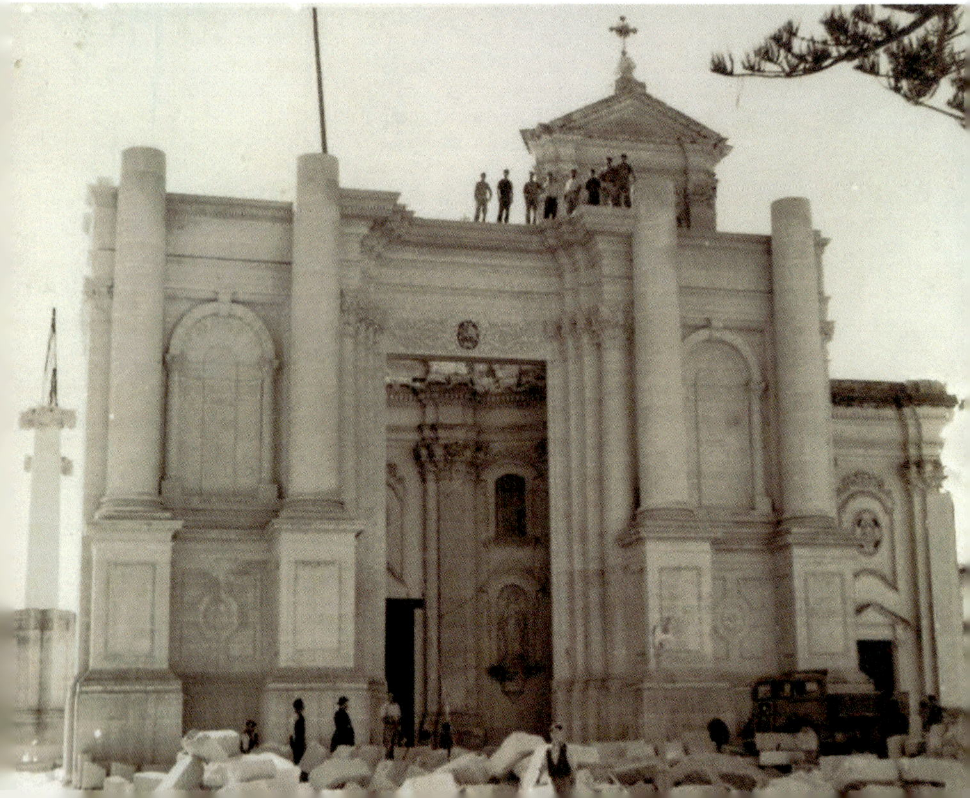

Several prosperous families led by Captain Orazio Mizzi, the three Farrugia Brothers, *t'Għakrex*, Felić Grech *ta' Marjanu*, Magro Brothers, and Dr. Giuseppe Pace LL.D., the latter from Sliema, Malta came forward. All pledged to pay the generous sum of 500 pounds sterling for the five of the eight reinforced concrete columns, on which the mighty dome would rest.

The fishermen and the merchants of Xewkija joined forces and also rose to the occasion; both generously donated one column each, respectively. Government employees plucked up courage and collectively pledged to fork out two and a half shillings every week from their paycheck until they raised the princely sum of 500 pounds sterling to make good for the eighth column.

However, that was not all. To guarantee that work would not stop for lack of funds, the existing seven hundred families bound themselves (although not obliged) to pay one shilling a week for as long as work went on uninterruptedly.

The first man on the right behind the three boys, is Guzepp Cauchi, the first master mason who laid the foundations of the Rotunda church

In itself this was also a milestone and a great achievement. The ever tireless and enterprising Pawlu Grech was behind this genial idea. Pawlu always argued that with 'his' shilling the church will not be built, but with 'everyone's contribution' it can be constructed. Like Carlyle, Pawlu firmly believed that *"The wealth of man is the number of things which he loves and blesses which he is loved and blessed by".*

Friar Fonz Farrugia together with another patriot from Xewkija, Salvu Haber *tal-Vixxni* who were in Australia also made a substantial collection.

The Pontifical Commission of Sacred Art from Rome forwarded the plans of the church to Bishop Pace. These were designed by engineer D'Amato and subsequently examined and approved *cum Laude*, according to Sacred Art. The permits were issued on 13 November 1951 by the Building Control Board and forwarded to Archbishop Pace with the registered number 3989/51 and 6549/47, respectively.

On 25 November 1951 archpriest Grech made another heartfelt appeal:

The formidable façade taking shape

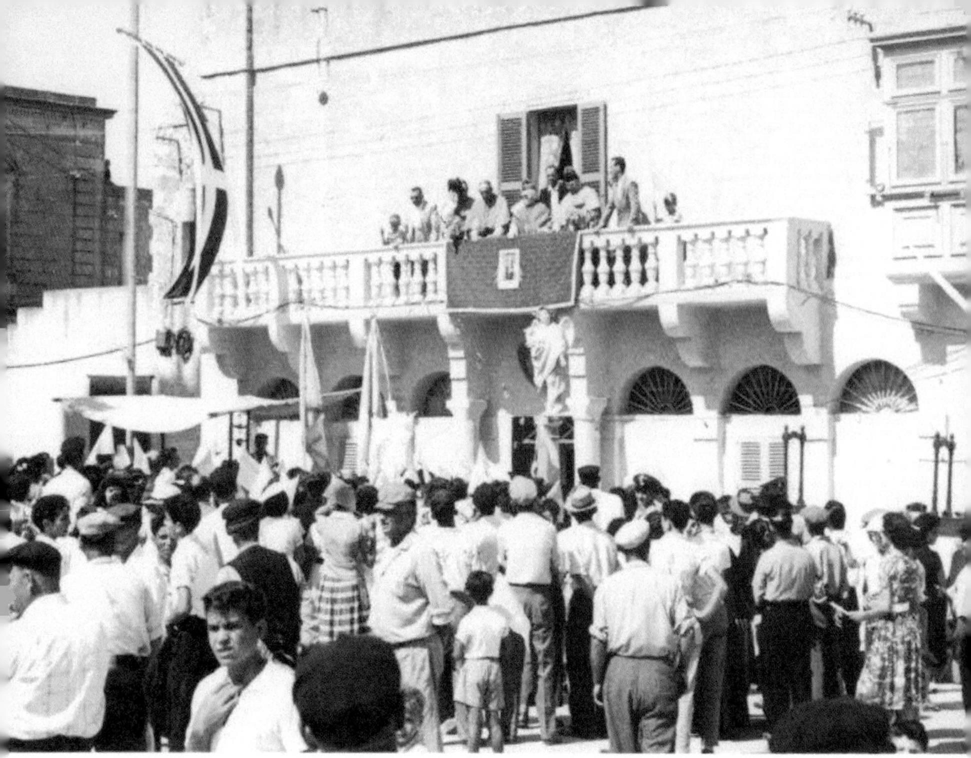

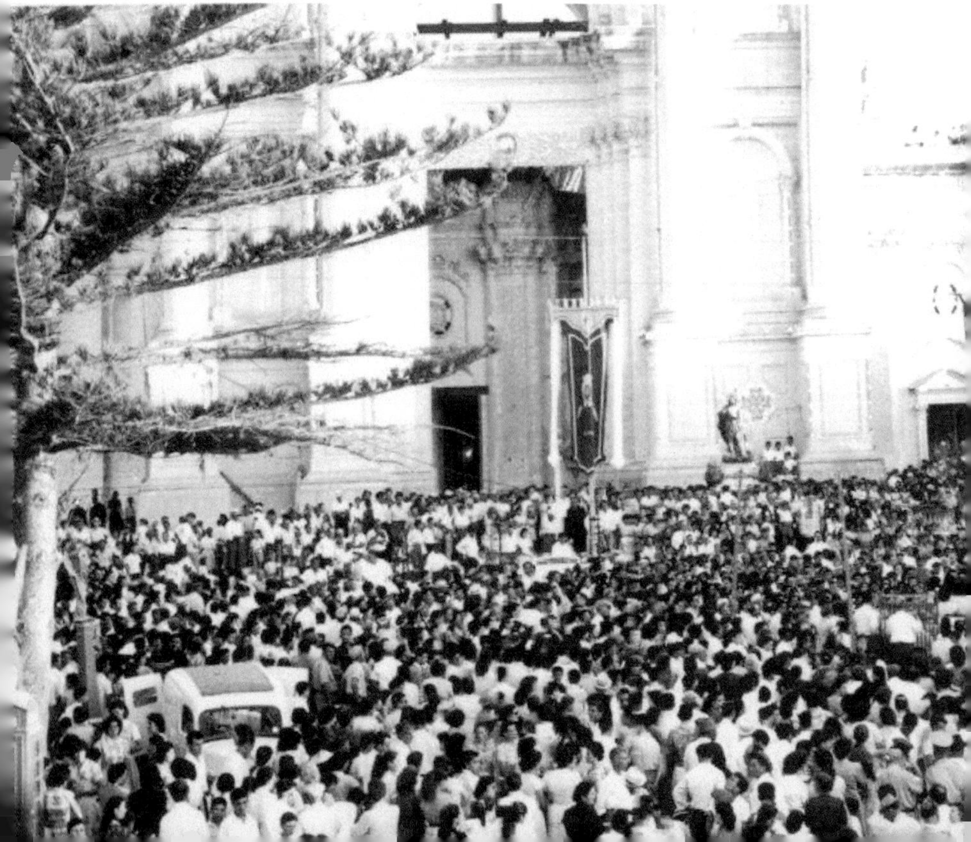

"I am pleased to inform you, that with the help of God and our Protector St. John, work is to commence on the new church.

"Therefore, it is required that everyone help both with money, according to what he can afford, as well as with work.

"Now it is necessary, that everyone gives his/her share to the building of our church, especially the fishermen, by donating one-third to St. John, and those who breed sows, can give their share as well, so that St. John will look after their livestock.

"Contact your families who are overseas and inform them of the task of building our church, so that we will not spend all that we have collected and come to an abrupt halt. If everyone helps, with one thing or another, we can complete our task without ever stopping.

"Now, the Bishop has not only granted permission for work to be done on Sundays and during feast days on the church but wants that every Sunday, you decide who is to start coming and giving a hand and finishing whatever is needed in the construction. This way you will save much money for the church.

"There is the need this morning to clear the rocks behind the church from the stones and soil so that tomorrow Mr. D'Amato can lay the stones for the foundation of the new church.

"Therefore, this morning at 8.00 a.m. those men who can come to give us a helping hand, can bring their spade, shovel, and pick ax, bucket, cart or truck.

Now it depends on you. If you help, we can move forward... Remember that what you do is done for God and St. John, and not for people's sake.

"The Bishop gave us permission to start building because he believes that everyone can give a helping hand and pitches in as best as he can. And be certain, that St. John will intercede for those who will help in this deed so that Jesus will hold a place in heaven for his eternal rest."

Thus began the toil of clearing the rubble to make way for the huge foundations of the new church. Volunteers wasted

The old church dwarfed by the new one

no time in clearing away all the stones with their mules and donkey carts.

Others hauled and loaded their small trucks with all the rubble and crushed stone in wicker baskets, while many an able *Xewki*, joined and offered a helping hand. Wooden pulleys were used to haul up the larger stones.

Human brawn and sweat were primarily provided by a whole battalion of men, women and children who were organized into regimental groups to perform this laborious task.

With untiring diligence and unstinting work of shoveling and carting soil in wicker baskets, leveling rocks and clearing crushed stones, the foundation ground was now ready for the laying of the first stone of the amazing Rotunda.

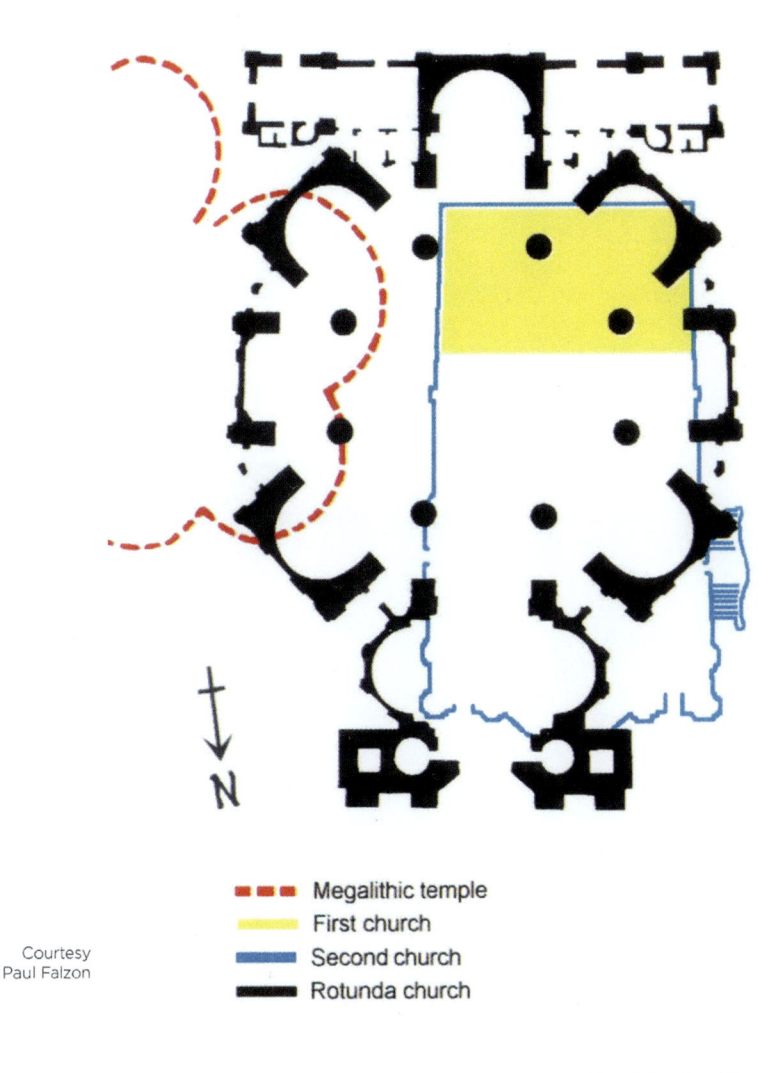

- - - Megalithic temple
▬ First church
▬ Second church
▬ Rotunda church

Courtesy
Paul Falzon

The Rotunda - 53

The Laying of the First Stone by Archbishop Pace - May 4, 1952

Chapter five

A Born Genius

*"Their fathers' great wish
and their greatest joy."*
The inscription placed on the main door of the church.

*"We are what we repeatedly do; excellence, then,
is not an act but a habit."*

Aristotle

Since architect Ġuze' D'Amato was a great devout of St. Joseph, he wanted that work on the new church starts on the 19th of March. He always started all his major projects on this particular day, and none of his works failed.

Born in Tunisia in 1886 of Maltese parents, at 19 he came to Malta but went back to Tunis to continue his studies in architecture.

In 1929, D'Amato returned to Malta and designed some churches and large buildings in a style that could be deemed classic. Two of his graceful churches are those of Kalkara and Raħal Ġdid, respectively.

The latter is a large classic church where he introduced some arches held by concrete columns covered in local limestone. It enhanced the church with a Roman architectonic effect.

In his book, 'Fortress – Architecture and Military History in Malta', Professor Quentin Hughes, wrote that, *"It is to men like Damato, that the credit must go for maintaining a tradition palatable to Malta until she produces a generation of architects capable of adapting modern architecture ..."*

On 5 January 1952, the Head of the Government Sanitary Department sent the building license to architect Giuseppe Refalo and archpriest Giuseppi Grech of Xewkija, simultaneously.

Fifteen men loading a truck from the first quarry in Xewkija, south of Ta' Lambert. Santa Cecilia/ Ta' Macedonia tower can be seen on the upper left hand side.

The eastern part of the church was used as our unofficial playing field

The Rotunda in 1956 when Master Mason Gużepp Vella probably took over from Gużepp Cauchi

The ceremony during the Blessing of the First Stone

Part of the large crowd during the Feast of the Baptist

Emigrants on holiday taking part in the feast of The Baptist around the year 1955

Construction on the side of St Zachary Street

Steel rods jutting out from one of the main arches Behind is the base for the Cupola already in place

This license implicitly stated that works can be carried out on the church of Xewkija according to the plans of D'Amato. The document bears No. 241/51 and is signed by Perit Giuseppe Refalo.

So the first stone was solemnly laid on 4 May 1952 by His Excellency Monsignor Ġużeppi Pace Bishop of Gozo. It was a glorious day for Xewkija. Bells rang joyously and flags fluttered from practically every rooftop. Bishop Pace was triumphantly welcomed amidst the vast enthusiasm of people who flocked from all over the village and beyond.

People clapped and kneeled reverently, toward His Excellency Bishop Pace. A large crowd gave loud applause and happily waved flags, palm fronds, and placards, with incisions bearing the words, *Viva l- Papa, Viva l'Isqof, Viva l-Arċipriet Grech u l-Kleru tax-Xewkija.*

The bishop's car was pulled with ropes from the octagonal windmill built during the time of Grand Master Perellos, all the way up Racecourse Street, (now Independence Street) to the main square. He was accompanied by a squad of nine police officers on horseback and the dynamic, euphonious din of the Leone Band.

At 5.30 p.m. the bishop who was deeply impressed by the enthusiasm of the *Xewkin* placed and blessed the 'First Stone'. It weighed one ton. In a particular hole, he placed a couple of silver and gold coins together with several saints' medals in a glass tube with a parchment written to mark this important occasion.

The godfathers for the blessing and the laying of the first stone were Captain Orazio Mizzi and Magro Brothers. The witnesses were Chevalier Edgar Montanaro, Gozo Commissioner, Dr. A. Tabone, Superintendent of Victoria Hospital, Chevalier Lorenzo Zammit Haber, Mr. Carlo Galea, Proprietor of Pax Flour Mills, and Architect Giuseppe D'Amato.

The celebrations continued until nightfall. The village was lit like a bonfire with candles aux flambeaux, torchlights, and electric bulbs. From top to bottom the whole façade of the old church was lit up, and the artistic statue of the Baptist was carried out of its niche.

Closing one of the 16 windows big enough for a double-decker bus to pass through it.

Two of the columns now in place

60 - The Rotunda

The giant Norfolk Island pine tree (*Araucaria heterophylla*), planted in the square that rose up to 24.3 meters (80 feet), was lit up with electric bulbs in different colors. It was the first time in Gozo, and the tree could be clearly visible from Marfa, Malta.

The people of Xewkija gave full vent to their immense joy. At last their wish, after waiting a whole generation to build a new church, was granted. The beaming archpriest held a small reception at the parish house for the distinguished guests.

On the main door of the church the following inscription was placed:

Today
Fourth of May of the year 1952
Together with the people of Xewkija let there be joy in the hearts of all Maltese of Malta and Gozo
Because during this Kingdom of great usefulness
Of Pope Pius XII and Elizabeth the Second of England
His Excellency Ġuzeppi Pace, Bishop of Gozo
With many beautiful Degrees and with the Cross of the Order of St. John, strengthened
This First Stone
Blessed and laid in its place
Therefore, this Monument started
Selected and alone
With the skill of Man and Belief in God
Drawn by the Most Recognized Architect Ġuze' D'Amato
Temple Adorned with Columns
In Honor of St. John the Baptist, Patron of this City
Strong Defender of Malta and Gozo
That today the people of Xewkija together with their Clergy
With their most resourceful Archpriest Ġuzeppi Grech United
With their enthusiastic hearts and with open hands
The work started that was
Their fathers' great wish
and their greatest joy.

Work started in earnest under chief masons' Ġużepp Cauchi *tas-Sellieħ*, and Toni Vella *tal-Malla*, both from Xewkija. They worked together for the first four and a half years.

The old dome inside the new church

The 'custom made lathe'. First from left is master mason Toni Vella, Nisju Tabone and his brother George.

For each column 300 bags of cement and one and two third tons of iron were used. They rise up 13.5 meters (45 feet).

One of the eight columns being prepared before it is encased in concrete and eventually covered in stone. One column cost 500 pounds sterling.

A pillar in the aisle of the old church.

The choir arch

The Rotunda - 63

In the beginning, the stones were quarried from a quarry in Xewkija, south of *ta' Lambert*, and then from the village of Sannat called *tal-Bur*, and later, from the village of Għarb. *Ta' Randu* operated the Għarb quarry. This quarry yielded a vastly superior type of stone.

Randu's son recounted to the writer how archpriest Grech used to visit their house at Għajn Mhelhel Street, in Żebbuġ. Grech carried a WWII American CARE (Cooperative for Assistance and Relief Everywhere) rice bag, that was used as a pouch full of pennies and halfpennies to settle the invoices. It used to take Randu's family a whole morning to count the pennies and the occasional gleaning shilling!

It is not surprising particularly since archpriest Grech paid Randu every six months. From the receipts that the writer examined, each bill amounted to around three or four hundred pounds sterling. *Ta' Randu* supplied the rest of the stones until the very end, many a times at a special, discounted price.

Chief mason Toni Vella concentrated with the utmost precision on the building of the eight Corinthian columns, four of which shot up from inside the old church, one of them right through an apse. The latter posed a tremendous challenge and a significant risk.

Since the size of the stone for these columns was enormous, George Tabone *ta' Gurġuna*, acquired a lathe from Malta Dockyard. George ingeniously adapted the lathe whereby these large and heavy stones were rotated and carved on a horizontal axis. Remnants of this lathe are today exhibited in the church museum, on level 3.

Consequently, this gave chief mason Toni Vella and his laborers the flexibility to shape and cut the stone into a perfect shape with amazing efficiency. In the process, this meant that not only work did not slacken, but they saved much valuable time.

Żakkarija Cilia and his laborers prepared the twelve 13.5 meters (45 feet) long, one inch thick rods that were placed inside these columns. They were assisted by George and his brother Dionisju, better known as Nisju.

These rods were in turn tied with another iron belt every 10 centimeters (4 inches). For each column, 300 bags of cement and one and two third tons of iron were used. Two men could not even embrace the width of the column.

As the church edifice clearly began to take shape, chief mason Cauchi who had just completed the beautiful choir, realized that this was his swansong, as his health was failing him. It was partly due to his age and partly to being overwhelmed with such a pressing project. Laying stones, some weighing over a ton, some the size of a Victorian desk, certainly took its toll on him.

Ġuże' D'Amato, who by now was also the architect in charge of the building of St. Joseph's Institute, poached the young and energetic Ġuzepp Vella *tal-Malla*, from this site. Ġużepp was Toni's little brother.

Ġużepp was the master mason building the edifice mentioned above on Mġarr Road, Għajnsielem. Without further ado, D'Amato took him to Xewkija. This shrewd move proved to be D'Amato's most notable coup.

D'Amato fully well knew and acknowledged as much that Ġużepp was a born genius, and he was not going to let him get out of his sight. Sure, this was a hard brief, but D'Amato was convinced that Ġużepp could fulfill it with equanimity.

Ġużepp started working alongside Cauchi. Chief mason Cauchi, who had decades of experience under his belt, understood immediately that this young lad was a *figlio d'arte*, par excellence.

After four and a half years laying all the foundations from the ground up, chief mason Cauchi left Ġużepp fully in charge.

Ġużepp never looked back. He stood on the shoulder of giant mason Cauchi and continued building upon his solid foundations. Ġużepp tackled and solved the problem of the middle column without removing the apse of the old church so as not to interrupt religious functions.

Otherwise, the old dome would have fallen apart. He did this by placing two steel beams with heads resting on the old church and then built fifteen courses up until the whole church was finished.

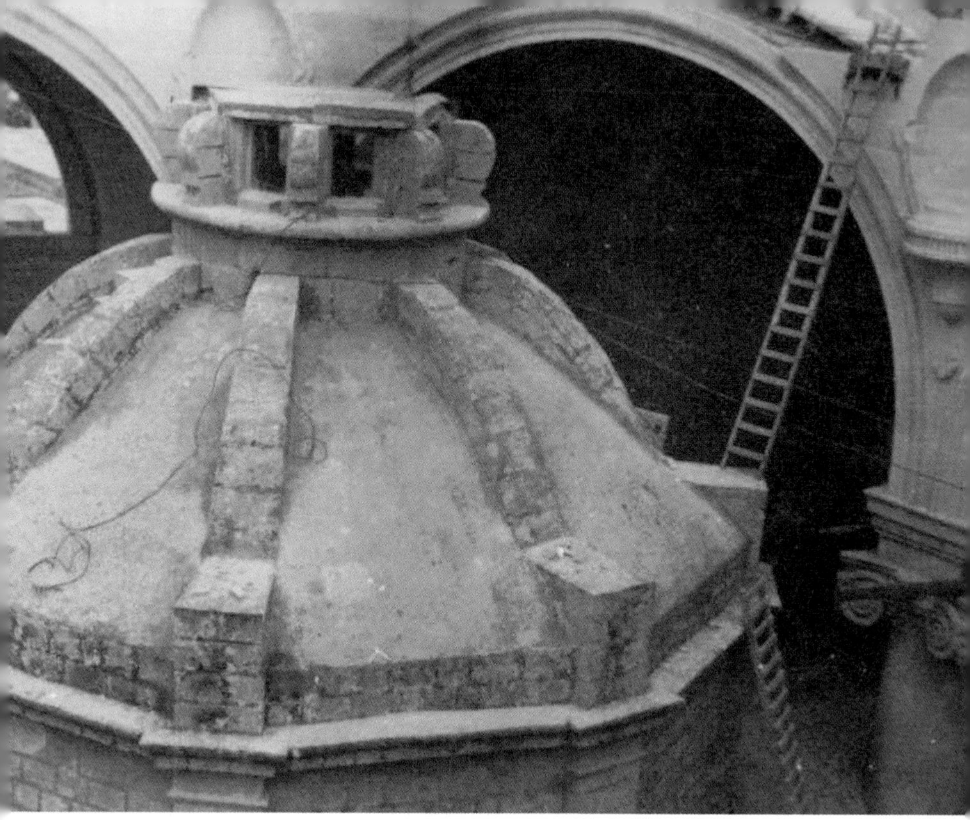

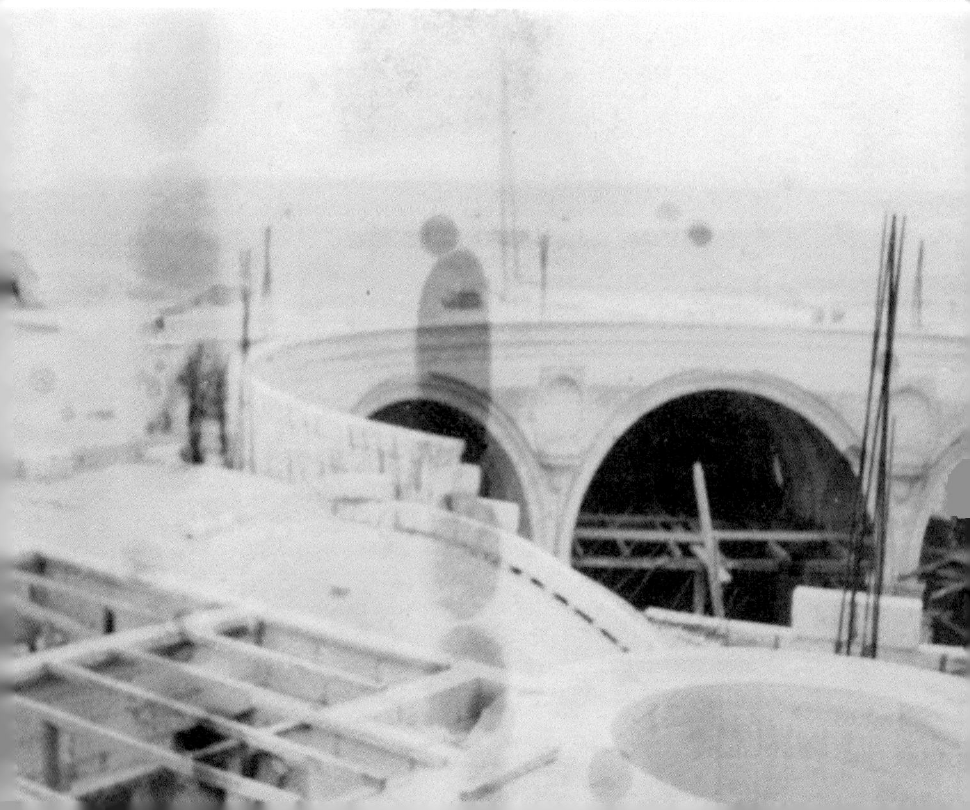

Afterward, with due attention and extreme caution, he dismantled the old church, dislocating stone by stone and built from the ground up the half column until it joined with the rest of the structure. It was just brilliant. Ġużepp *tal-Malla* knew exactly what he was doing.

Ġużepp had a loyal and trusted team of excellent stone dressers and carvers. His brother-in-law, Victor Haber *ta' Gurġun*, spearheaded them. These were Ġanni Vella *ta' Lobu*, Feliċ Spiteri *tal-Pisklu*, Emmanuel Haber *ta' Ferris*, Ġużepp Attard and his brother Ġanni *tal-Ħass*, Frenċ Xerri *ta' Xmun*, Salvu Xuereb *tas-Sajku*, Ġużepp Zammit *tar-Rest*, Emmanuel Attard *tas-Sinjura*, Mikieli Spiteri *taċ-Ċaċċ*, and Vitor Cini and his son Ġanni *ta' Bibellu*, among others.

These men were some of the best dedicated stone dressers on the island. Their work was doubly hard since most of the stones were so big and heavy that it was not possible to lift them up onto another stone and thus ease themselves a little bit upwards.

Top of the old dome
Heavy wooden ladders were widely used during the construction of the church

It would have mitigated and relieved the stone carver from having to bend all the way down to do the work on these massive stones. It certainly was backbreaking.

One of these stone carvers, still living, recounted to the writer that sometimes, after eating lunch, the bread was back in his mouth after stooping down so low to work on the stones. Obviously, their heads were always pointing downwards.

Heartened by the indomitable progress, archpriest Grech was joined with the rest of his clergy.These were Dun Ġwann Xuereb *tal-Bilbel*, Dun Ġwann Grech *ta'Marjanu*, Mgr., Carmelo Bajada *tal-Faħam*, Dun Anton Xuereb *tal-Lenċa*, and Dun Karm Azzopardi *ta' Ġeremija*, whom all took turns knocking at every household. They collected the one shilling that the villagers bound themselves to give so that work would not come to a standstill.

Preparations well underway for the Golden Ring

Later, these clergymen were unfailingly joined by others, including Dun Ġużepp Camilleri *ta' Sika*, and Dun Ġwann Attard *tas-Sekk*. Rain or shine, week in and week out, year after year, every Wednesday or Thursday, the archpriest and his assistants led the way to collect the promised shilling or sixpence. Alternatively, a dozen eggs from

The Rotunda - 67

Ġużepp Cauchi		Ġużepp Vella		Toni Vella

One of the side columns that could not be finished before the old church was taken down

68 - The Rotunda

those families who could least afford it. The indefatigable Dun Ġwann Xuereb, who was also the assistant pastor, joined the clergy.

Weekly wages amounted to around 80 pounds sterling, which was over four thousand pounds sterling per annum. Then there was the stone, gravel and sand, fuel, cement, and other related expenses to pay. The last shipment of iron rods obtained from wholesale merchants amounted to 1,100 pounds sterling.

Meanwhile, merchants of animal fodder, milk, and alcohol, together with poultry breeders, were all urged to chip in. Farmers laid aside part of their profit from their produce. Shopkeepers and grocery store owners placed metal tins on their counters to collect donations.

Fishermen laid aside as much as one-third of their profit as part of the proceeds for the building of the new church. Families who had a shed or a chicken coop in their back garden raised an extra chick or cock or a moorhen; similarly those who bred rabbits raised an additional bunny or two.

Lace-makers set aside a couple of their fine table cloths and Irish linen doilies. These were raffled in lotteries under the auspices of Dun Ġwann Xuereb, Dun Ġwann Grech or Pawlu Grech, besides other helpers.

Pawlu's sister Marija *ta' Bejża* was also a fervent and energetic fundraiser. She always volunteered to give a helping hand. Marija was later awarded '*Gieħ Ix-Xewkija*', the villages' highest honor that is conferred by the Mayor of Xewkija. To further raise funds, there were three principal lotteries held throughout each year. The prizes consisted of livestock such as a kid goat, fowls, home-reared lamb and pork, lace, jewelry, toys and other items ideal for the house.

The first lottery was on New Year's Day, the other just before the feast of St. John and the third one, on 29th August, the martyrdom of the Baptist.

Another two church collections were held: one at the end of the Lenten sermons (usually during the month of March) and the other during the Christmas novena sermons in early December.

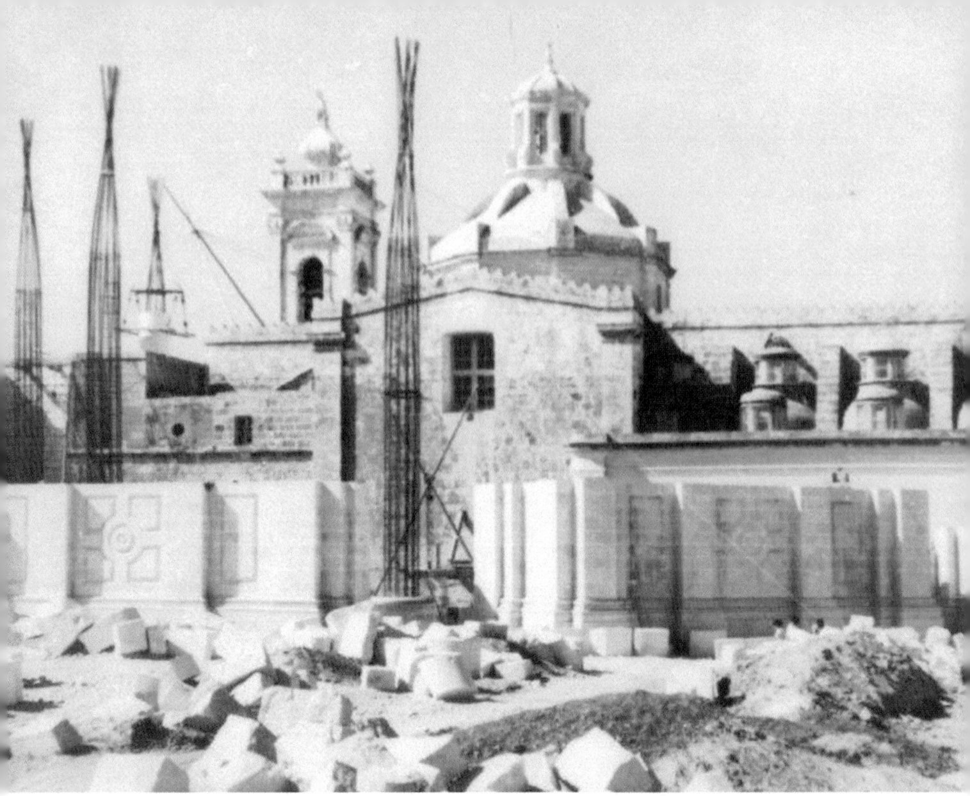

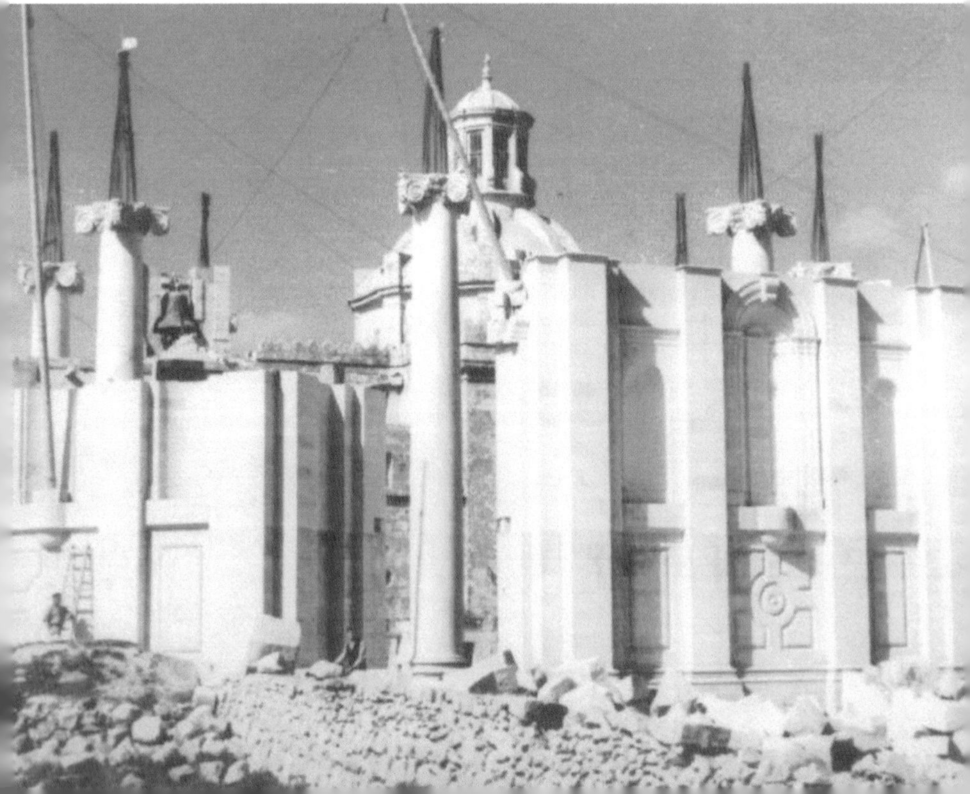

It is worth noting, that although thousands of miles away, Xewkija emigrants in Australia, North America, Canada, England and other countries, always forwarded *strina*, cash gifts. Tourists who visited the colossal church under construction felt impelled to chip in a coin or two.

Years later, when the Industrial Estate in Xewkija was up and running, many men, and most particularly young women from Xewkija, gave substantial contributions from their wages. These women worked for companies like Bluebell/Wrangler, Career Apparel, General Instrument, Mary Farrin and others.

Then one day a terrific explosion was heard with a roar like thunder coming from the sacristy of the church. The earth rocked, and a pall of smoke rose while an acrid gelignite smell enveloped the surrounding area.

It was a tragic fireworks explosion. Sadly, there was one victim, Pawlu Vella *ta' Ġilent*, who in his spare time, was preparing the annual feast's petards. Festivities were canceled, and the whole village mourned the 23-year-old patriot. It happened on 14 May 1960.

The old church completely encircled by the new one.

9 July 1969
Royal Visit to Xewkija New Church.

Prince Charles and his sister Princess Anne on the parvis of the old church being welcomed by Archpriest Grech, Sir Maurice Dorman, the last British Governor - General of Malta is on the right
Courtesy Grech Studio

72 - The Rotunda

Chapter Six

Golden Ring

Our poetic "destiny" was replaced by the discovery of an aristocracy deeper and older. We were builders.
Confessions of Fausto Maijstral

"History," *Dnubietna wrote,* "is a step-function."
V. by Thomas Pynchon.

Master mason Vella always hoped for the great assistance and unlimited bounty of the Lord. He had a devoted wife and seven siblings. Almost every day started with his participation in the first Mass at four thirty in the morning. It helped him concentrate on an oncoming day.

Ġużepp was utterly focused and determined to achieve this goal. He never relented in his great zeal to finish this giant project he was entrusted. Whenever he was approached by third parties to do other outside work, he would promptly refuse the offer.

His primary concern and only mission then were to finish the church. Since no stone was the same like another, he cut and made all the patterns and forms that were required. During the entire edifice, an incredible 1,600 patterns were used.

When architect D'Amato asked him from where he got them, Ġużepp smiled and candidly replied that he adapted them from the sketches. D'Amato was extremely pleased since these turned out to be faultless.

Every stone fitted perfectly with each other. D'Amato could observe with his own eyes the excellent workmanship of every cut made by the expert stone-dressers. He noticed the lines at the edge of a barrel vault and the archivolt and in between courses were all the same, in precise linear symmetry. There was an essential characteristic: an emphasis on unity and balance among diverse but accurate parts.

Ġużepp would not cut corners or lay a single stone that was not cut to measure. There were no ifs or buts. His word and precision reigned supreme.

In his magisterial book entitled, 'Management: Tasks, Responsibilities, Practices', Professor Peter F. Drucker, who has been described as the founder of modern management, relates this episode:

'An old story tells of three stonecutters who were asked what they were doing. The first replied, 'I am making a living.' The second kept on hammering while he said, 'I am doing the best job of stonecutting in the entire country.' The third one looked up with a visionary gleam in his eyes and said, 'I am building a cathedral.'

The third man is, of course, master mason Ġużepp Vella *tal-Malla*.

The corbels or the frontispiece as it is also known took two years and two thousand two hundred truckloads of stones. It is worked out at one hundred twenty-five stones per truckload. All the stone was pure *globiġerina* limestone and of the same color. Twenty-five stones then cost one pound sterling and ten shillings.

The corners of the cornice of the flat arch in the façade consist of massive stones measuring 1.5 meters (5 feet) long and a width of .45 meters ($1^{1/2}$ feet).

To build this triumphal arch, master mason Vella obtained outriggers on loan from the Water Works Department. These were in turn screwed and tightened with steel vents. Later, workers poured a ship of concrete and iron so that Vella could build the frieze and cornice on top of it.

Meanwhile, the first three or four huge heads of the cornices resting on top and sprouting out from the eight columns around the church were sculpted by none other than Maestro Carmelo Micallef of Hamrun, Malta. The rest were all done brilliantly by another Maestro, Toni Camilleri *tal-Gims*, from Xewkija.

These cornices or capitals are a delightful work of art. When Maestro Micallef left, Toni took over and carved all the rest of the other *kapitelli* just as masterfully. *Tal-Gims* has, in fact, the lion's share of all the great stone sculpture in the church. *Tal-Gims* family is extraordinarily good at elevating stone sculpture into the realm of the extraordinary. It is a hallmark of their trade to make the whole process look effortless.

Today, visitors and tourists stand in awe and wonder at the greatness of their beauty and of the Maltese stone itself. Moreover, these massive sculpted stones matched exactly and precisely with the frontispiece and the cornice. Jutting out and hanging high in the air, they are indeed a masterpiece.

Master mason Vella insisted that certain pieces of work be done solely by one hand. For instance, many of the frontispieces and entablatures were carved by Felić Spiteri *tal-Pisklu*.

The next challenge was the eight lunettes. A lunette is formed when a horizontal cornice transects a round-headed arch at the level of the imposts, where the arch springs. No one knew how these 'half-moons', were going to be closed, including architect D'Amato, who at one point suggested that perhaps he should just cover the area with a simple and plain concrete roof.

The amiable D'Amato occasionally supervised the on-going work from a dangling wicker basket, hoisted high, high up in the air by a motor winch. However, Ġużepp ruled it out. He had another clever idea how to build it. He started two lunettes in a V-shaped form from the bottom until they met each other and formed a little dome.

Each and every single stone had to be carved, 'bended' and shaped in such an undulating way that was nothing short of perfection. It called for a mind of supreme intelligence and the workmanship and skill of a real craftsman. Amazingly, Ġużepp joined the first two lunettes together in less than a week.

Master mason Vella telephoned D'Amato and kindly asked him to come and take a look so that he could determine if the former should continue building them this way. It was a wet and cold winter, and the architect who was now in his mid-seventies, would not dare cross the channel during inclement weather. D'Amato was physically a well-built man and of great stature but suffered badly from bouts of seasickness.

The old church being dismantled stone by stone.

Every single stone was meticulously numbered and rebuilt in the Museum of Sculpture exactly as it stood in the old shrine

Two volunteers helping out

On the third week, the weather relented. The sky opened up, the sun came out, and the sea calmed down so that the veteran architect managed to cross the Gozo channel and make a site inspection.

With one hand holding a handkerchief to his mouth as he was still suffering as a result of the ferry crossing, D'Amato looked up and was completely blown away by what he saw.

Felić Spiteri was one of the stone carvers present that day. He recounted to the writer that D'Amato went down on both knees with gratitude and appreciation of how beautiful and perfected these lunettes turned out to be. D'Amato quickly called Ġużepp to clamber down and told him in front of all the workers present, that from now on there was no need for him as an architect to supervise the building anymore.

D'Amato was so pleased and impressed with this master piece, that from then onwards he left master mason Vella fully in charge of the entire edifice. The huge arches underneath the dome are all curved and shaped in the form of a circle. From these columns sprout another four arches: two small and two bigger. These are the spandrels between the arch and the drum of the dome at the crossing of the church.

When one looks from underneath these arches, one gets the impression or at least the perception that these are going to fold down. If these were not curved, the dome would have instead turned out in the form of a metal nut, that is, octagonal like that of Santa Maria della Salute in Venice.

Instead, Ġużepp, ever loyal to D'Amato's plans, undertook significant efforts to build it round. Obviously, this called for and required a tremendous amount of precision, skill and time, which result can be very well seen and appreciated today. These eight pairs of compass arches took 90 bags of cement each and seven and a half tons of iron to undertake.

The seven shells in the form of a cockle turned out to be another impressive piece de resistance. Vitor Vella *tal-Qanfuda*, a well-known master mason from Żebbug, who built a few like shells for the gorgeous Basilica of

The wire tied to the winch, that was used to haul up most of the material

The steel wire net was decisive in the finishing of the Dome

One of the eight columns rising through the old church

Ta' Pinu, admired them greatly. So did several renowned British architects.

These skilled and distinguished professional peers openly wondered about the precision of these fine lines, and at how these shells were immaculately executed. Each one was a true masterpiece.

George Tabone, who was a highly experienced carpenter by trade, helped out again, this time, by building three wooden forms. He assisted master Vella with the arches above the choir so that the master mason could connect one arch with another perfectly.

Wooden planks were brought, and a bonfire started at the back of the sacristy for these planks to be curved and bended accordingly. The planks were placed above a crackling fire and tied at each end with screws; these were constantly rotated and wetted with water so as not to burn the plank itself.

Once these were shaped and formed and the curve set in, the planks were unscrewed slowly to make sure that the curve stayed correctly as desired. Later, these wooden forms were used for the construction of the arches. The curve was 76.2cms (two and a half feet) deep. With this precious help, master mason Vella was able to close the three major arches to perfection as well.

Several people thought that these arches fell outside the diameter, but, in fact, these are one hundred percent in the form of a compass. D'Amato himself had confirmed this before he passed away at the age of 77, on 26 May 1963.

Many people paid their respects to this eminent architect at his funeral. A street in Xewkija and the Boys Secondary School in Raħal Ġdid are today named after him. One day, D'Amato chatting with the workers smilingly said, *"If it were possible by a wild stretch of imagination to make a helicopter lift up the Church from the cross, the whole dome together with the eight ferroconcrete columns, would come up intact, so strongly are all parts united."*

On 12 July of the same year, Perit Joseph Mizzi *tas-Swejs*, from San Lawrenz, signed his name at the office of P.H. Department as the architect in charge of the works being carried out at the Xewkija church. A few months later,

Heavy steel beams were widely used during the construction of the church

The closing of the last window

Sixteen windows ready for the dome

Perit Mizzi was appointed as Director, Civil Engineer & Architect with the Public Works Department in Gozo.

Next in line were the shells of the side chapels such as the one where Our Lady of Rosary is today. Once a bet was made that master mason Vella could close it within five days.

It required building 39 courses, and indeed this was finished successfully. Ġużepp had the fantastic ability to draw and sketch a thing in his mind as to how he was going to construct it. More than a genius, he was a visionary.

When archpriest Grech used to ask him how he was going to do this particular piece of work, his frank answer would be that he was already visualizing it finished. *"Genius,"* Ruskin once remarked, *"is only a superior power of seeing."*

Once, the writer recalls, Ġanni Vella, *ix-Xagħri*, who was giving a helping hand, got stuck midway when he was building the winding, spiral *garigor* staircase. It is in the narthex, on the immediate left-hand side of the façade, as one enters the church through the main door. It rises to a height of some 18 meters (60 feet). Ġanni sent one of his sons to fetch his brother Toni.

Saturday morning turned out a fine, warm day, with a pure cloudless sky. At around 10 o'clock, a group of volunteers were helping Żakkaria Cilia pull a thick rough rope to hoist the large stone slabs that Ġanni was placing as part of the unsupported winding stairs.

Toni came right over since his house was nearby, in the vicinity where Gourgion tower once stood. Quiet and reserved Toni first listened, his head cupped in his hand in a thoughtful mode.

The smoke from a cigarette filtered slowly upwards, in a serpentine way. There was complete silence. Nobody said a word. One could hear a church mouse fart.

Then, after a brief exchange between the two brothers, the problem was resolved with a minimum of fuss. It was done by replacing and alternating a couple of stones.

Żakkarija and the rest of the volunteers resumed hoisting

The Rotunda around 1968

Preparing for the Dome

The Dome well underway

up the remaining heavy stone slabs so that Ġanni eventually completed the spiral stairway all the way up to the roof level, successfully. Then the big day arrived. This day will not easily be forgotten in the history of Xewkija, a day that called for the whole village to come out and give a helping hand.

Archpriest Grech implored all able-working men to leave Saturday 16 July, free so that they could take part in the greatest scheme of the church. The year was 1964, the same year when two months later, Malta became Independent.

The ring formed part of the circular drum that is interposed between pendentive and dome, which inevitably gave the hemispherical dome, greater elevation. The pendentive is a triangular section of a vaulting rising from the angle of two walls to support a dome.

It called for the laying of the reinforced concrete ring that needed tons and tons of concrete to be poured all in one day. The ring itself was of massive proportions, one and a half meter (5 feet) deep, and one and a half meter wide.

Temporary platforms using steel beams were assembled. Some of these steel beams were acquired with the help of the late but never forgotten architect D'Amato, from the Dominican Sisters' Hospital, in Attard, Malta.

The ring was to tie the eight columns together and eventually bear the full, perpendicular weight of the entire dome. Inside, the ring was circled with 53.34cms (twenty-one-inch) iron rods, tied with a belt every 10 cms (four inches).

Petards were fired at four in the morning so that all volunteers would gather on time. Workers were divided into eight separate regiments; four groups on the ground with spades, hoes, mattocks, shovels and buckets to prepare and mix the concrete. Another four groups went on top of the ring itself to carry and cast the mortar.

Preparations for this major undertaking were carried out days before. Sand, gravel, aggregate and cement bags were prepared and positioned in place.

Master Mason Vella first from right working on the closing of the dome with Ninu Vella and Żakkarija Cilia
Courtesy Guza Vella

The *Xewkin* had, like squirrels in winter, stockpiled jerry cans filled with petrol and diesel fuel for the cement mixers and the motor winches. Several large tanks and special reservoirs stored water.

A fleet of old trucks full of sand and gravel and bowsers overflowing with water were on hand. A heavy Bedford and a Dodge vehicle the writer recalls belonging to Wenzu Borg *ta' Ġenju,* and Pawlu Spiteri *tal-Majru,* respectively were loaded with red sand.

A Leyland water bowser, owned by Emmanuel Vella *tal-Baħri,* was standing by to supply the water. There were many other pre-war trucks besides the ones mentioned, full to the brim with aggregate.

The main square of Xewkija was choked with machinery and looked like one huge beehive of a construction site. There were mounds of sand and hills of gravel and cement bags piled high in the air.

Traffic was diverted, and no one except those rendering a

service was allowed in during this operation, unofficially dubbed, "Golden Ring". There were no cranes then. Except for the cement mixers and the motor winches, everything else was done by hand. Four different sites, that is, north, south, east, and west, on an axis of equity distance around the church grounds were set up.

Altogether, there were four winches. These were tied to four symmetrical outriggers with a steel wire dangling to haul up the concrete tanks, the boilers or a wooden box that could hold up to sixteen iron pails at one go.

These were manned by local stone masons from Xewkija and included their 'guys', that is, their workers whom all volunteered to work for free that day. Benford cement mixers were stationed nearby. (The cost of one Benford mixer was one hundred fifty-five pounds sterling).

Similarly, four other sites parallel to the winches on top of the church were positioned and ready with men on platforms, holding wheelbarrows to carry and pour the concrete once it got up there.

The sixteenth of July is the feast of Our Lady of Mount Carmel. It proved to be a good omen. Perit Mizzi was hoisted up in a wicker basket on top of the ring. Mizzi gave strict instructions on the exact mix of the cement mortar in the ratio of 1:2:4. No one was to deviate from this mixture.

Work started feverishly at 5 am with mixers puttering away while motor winches stuttered, vigorously pulling the well-greased steel cables that wound around the revolving drums.

Scores of men, women and children scooped sand, shoveled gravel, split open cement bags or fetched buckets of water. Work went on unabated. The glaring summer heat did not deter the people from their excitement and enthusiasm to complain about the scorching July sun. They just wanted to get the job done.

Those men who got tired were promptly relieved and replaced by other willing volunteers. When sand or gravel was running low, trucks were immediately dispatched to Nadur, to cart more aggregate. Perit Mizzi directed those with wheelbarrows to pour the concrete back to

One of the eight columns almost finished

back so that eventually the concrete cast did not dry on them. This way all the concrete poured became one whole, solid ring. It was a simple but ingenious plan, nonetheless.

Exhaustion started to take its toll; hands drooped, knees became weak, and concentration was fast losing its acumen.

At around twelve thirty in the afternoon, as the sun was now high and directly in his face, the operator of the motor winch working on the western side of the sacristy started to slack. He hit and caught from underneath one of the steel beams with a large tank full of concrete. These 'loose' steel beams were used for the support of the scaffolding platform.

There were shouts and loud cries of "watch-out, watch-out", as the steel beam toppled and came roaring down hitting one wall against another. Naturally there were many people underneath but Divine Providence, far wiser and nobler than any human mind could ever have imagined, miraculously prevented the steel beam from hitting or injuring anyone.

An hour or so later, Kelinu Xerri *ta' Xmun*, who is the writer's first cousin, got hit by another swinging concrete boiler. He was on top of the ring platform.

Like all the other volunteers, he was unharnessed and not wearing a hard hat. Kelinu lost his balance and fell a height of about ten feet, mercifully missing a wide open port hole on the roof by a sheer couple of feet. He was barely scratched and could count his lucky stars.

After carting one thousand three hundred cement bags, shoveling mounds of sand, and gravel and fetching hundreds of buckets of water together with 10 tons of iron, the mammoth "Golden Ring" was finished by 7.15pm.

An enormous sigh of relief was given by the 250 fifty or so volunteers who worked from dawn to dusk, incessantly. When it dried, the ring was broad enough to drive a car over it. At the spur of the moment, a collection raised the sum of four hundred forty-three pounds sterling.

On their way home, Kelinu and his brother Ġużepp, along with their father Ġanni *ta' Xmun*, met Liberat, an old farmer. He carried a hoe slung over his shoulder, making his way up Racecourse Street, towards the church.

They told Liberat that "Golden Ring" was over. He could go home now. Old Liberat turned around and headed back. He was beside himself with joy.

Another sixteen windows (smaller) form the lantern

The wire net crisscrossing the dome.

Chapter Seven

The Dome

*Ring them bells, ye heathen
From the city that dreams
Ring them bells from the sanctuaries
'Cross the valleys and streams...*
                    Ring Them Bells by Bob Dylan

There is cause for rejoicing here. You may for a time have to suffer the distress of many trials; but this is so that your faith, which is more precious than the passing splendor of fire-tried gold, may by its genuineness lead to praise, glory and honor when Jesus Christ appears.
                    From the first letter of Peter 1:3-9

The dome presented its challenges. Not surprisingly, the higher one went up, the risks grew exponentially. The vast majority of work on the new church was done, day in and day out, by standing for hours on end, on a twelve-inch wide wooden plank. Sometimes, this was at a height of 21 meters (70 feet) or more.

One slip could be fatal. Some intrepid laborers even stood on upturned wooden soda crates. The work entailed was dangerous, and there was no warning, no yellow card for this high-wire act.

Master mason Vella was constantly cautious. For instance, if one had to strike a conversation with him in the middle of the square on a Sunday morning, before parting he would look down directly to the ground to ascertain exactly where he stood. That is how careful he was to maintain his balance.

To build the dome Ġużepp was confronted with a most difficult problem: how to create a platform from one end of the divide to the other. Initially, the late D'Amato had suggested they order special long steel beams from Malta Dockyard. These tie beams were to span the empty void of the enormous divide.

However, after several inquiries regarding the expenses involved, the quotation of the price for these tie beams came out to whopping four thousand pounds sterling.

The price was exorbitant. Ġużepp Vella thought he could build another church with that amount of money. So instead he went to Malta and brought back, loaded on a truck, sixty pounds sterling worth of steel wire. It turned out a work of engineering genius in any age.

Ġużepp devised a series of wires and vents from one end to another to form a net. One of his young laborers, his nephew, Ninu Vella *tar-Rapon*, bore vents the size of 3.81 centimeters (1.5 inches). These holes were bored through the stone and concrete to pass these cables through and then tightened them rigidly from outside, with heavy duty screws.

The steel wire had plastic so that it did not damage the stone. The cable itself was 3.81 centimeters thick and came in squares with clips. It was unyielding, so strong that this type of steel wire is used overseas for building big bridges.

Next, Ġużepp and his laborers did the frames and bolted them securely with screws. It became one huge steel net. Afterward, the workers spread an enormous blanket that was purposely bought from an awning of a commercial ship and tied it to the wires.

The steel net in turn was loaded with fifteen tons of wooden planks plus another twenty tons of stones. The steel net became as solid as the ground itself, and the more these wires were loaded, the firmer and more stable they became. Archpriest Grech thought this was an ingenious idea and was left open-mouthed, looking at the steel net. Ġużepp had singlehandedly saved the church an awesome fortune.

This cleverly contrived system proved to be the best flexible platform to work. Naturally, it was adopted and repeated every time it was required to go higher and higher, to eventually complete and close the dome.

This net also reduced the danger of the broad divide to the bare minimum. Except for one day. Storm clouds were gathering overhead and the wind was kicking up.

Then a violent gust of wind started blowing with unbelievable force from the west. It was so strong that the wind lifted the whole structure.

The wooden planks tied and fastened, heaved and creaked. Every thing else was tightly secured like a cord. However, as the cruel *punent* increased and blew forcefully, Ġużepp and his laborers thought the end was nigh and that they were going to be blown off with the whole platform and everything on it. The platform itself was huge and measured a diameter of 25.2 meters (83 feet).

The western wind blew through the sixteen, huge open windows. Each window has a reinforced concrete column with twelve steel rods, which rods are tied every 10 centimeters (4 inches).

These windows measure three meters (ten feet) wide and six meters (20 feet) high, large enough to drive a double-decker bus. Mercifully, the *punent* gale wind subsided, and no one was blown away. That was the scariest day.

Although Perit Mizzi was always on hand for any technical advice on a *pro bono* basis, master mason Vella had to work practically on his own. Żakkarija Cilia became his right-hand man. All they had now to rely on were just a few original sketches and drawings left by architect D'Amato.

Żakkarija was already in charge of the pointing and plastering and had proved to be an extremely able foreperson. He was the most senior worker since the church's inception, that is, 19 November 1951, from the very beginning of the laying of the foundations. He ended supervising all the pointing works on the Rotunda until its completion. His love and passion for the Rotunda and Xewkija itself knew no bounds.

Archpriest Grech trusted Żakkarija implicitly. It was archpriest Grech who had entreated Żakkarija not to emigrate to Australia and told him to wait until the permits were granted so that he would offer him a permanent job.

When master mason Vella began working on the architraves of these windows, which is essentially the

One of the intrepid workers abseiling with a rope and a prayer

Two barefoot workers laying the massive stone

The façade of the old church being dismantled.

92 - The Rotunda

vertical edge frame of the window, he thought of doing a bracket console around it and decorating it with an ornate ceiling fan.

This winning idea saved years of toil. So revolutionary this was that Ġużepp completed the work in three weeks flat. With regards to the actual planning of the dome, Ġużepp and Żakkarija took these sketches with them to the courtyard of Magro house, located across the street.

Neither Vella nor Cilia had gone to any Ivy League or any other university for that matter. They had no degrees in calculus or algebra and barely knew how to write their names. The 'step-function' that Ġużepp applied was that of a natural genius builder.

There, armed with a notebook, a flexible iron ruler, a pencil, and a piece of shoestring nailed into a wall, master mason Vella dictated, and Żakkarija noted. The dome was thus sketched from beginning to end, precisely and to the minutest detail. Everything matched beautifully, including the diameter.

The dome itself has sixteen columns and is chased with a channel. It is these columns that hold it together and support the sixteen windows. For each column, 20 sacks of cement and half a ton of iron were used. Over these columns, there is a second circle that required 500 sacks of cement and five tons of iron. Sixteen ribs protrude upwards from this second circle and reach up to 46 horizontal courses of stonework.

In each radiating rib, there is half a ton of vertical iron bars and one and one-fourth ton of iron was placed in each horizontal layer. Each layer took 200 sacks of cement.

There is a third circle joining the ribs together. 500 sacks of cement and one and two-thirds tons of iron were consumed. A further nine horizontal layers of stone took another 400 sacks of cement. Four tons of iron lead to the base circle of the lantern plus 600 sacks of cement and six and two-thirds tons of iron.

There are sixteen volutes around the dome. They look like buttresses but, in fact, are not so. This scroll-like ornament formed the basis of the Iconic order and was inspired by the curve of a ram's horn.

Two-tier steel net allowed great flexibility and more importantly safety, for Master Mason Vella and his workers.
The steel wire net that crisscrossed the dome proved to be the best flexible platform to work on.

These volutes with 'big ears' around the Rotunda, serve purely as an ornament, and do not hold or support the dome, at all. On top of these volutes are sixteen *pilandri*, a high vertical stone in the shape of an elegant slim triangle with a pinnacle pointing upwards, towards the open sky.

Master mason Vella was instrumental in the invention of a mounted cross-cut using a toothed blade to cut the stone. It is with this cross-cut that the whole dome was built. This power saw saved much time for this kind of work and was a great blessing.

Scores of children, including the writer and Toni Azzopardi *tal-Ħabib*, who had no acrophobia, would ask Ġużepp Attard *tal-Ħass*, to take us up in the same wooden box that he delivered stones and quarry powder. The latter was sieved and mixed with water until it was slushy for the master mason to use.

'Ask' is too kind a word. We would besiege him, begging Ġużepp to please hoist us up in the wooden box using the motor winch. Eventually, he would accede and haul us all the way up to the top of the platform.

Ġużepp Attard was shy, extremely kind and of a few words. He was powerful enough to lift a large stone from the ground up all by himself. He spent his life as the main stone-carrier from the very beginning. Thus, most of the stone passed through his giant hands and onto his shoulder.

Dressed and carved stones were laid down gently on damp sackcloth and wrapped like a tender baby, to prevent any chipping. Later, as his strength diminished, Ġużepp was in charge of sieving the quarry powder and putting it in buckets for the master mason to lay the stones.

Ġużepp, a jovial bachelor with a flushed face and radiating eyes, was always ready to help. Every time the writer steps into the Rotunda, Ġużepp's presence is felt as if he is still right there by the middle left column, near the side chapel. He is silently mixing the yellowish quarry powder with his mattock or otherwise operating the motor winch with his hand the size of one of Popeye's, resting on the green iron lever. May the Good Lord bless his soul.

His finest moment – Archpriest Ġużeppi Grech on the right accompanied by the Apostolic Nunzio, G. Maioli, chauffeured by Lorry Spiteri in a Ford Thunderbird on 31st May 1970

First from left Mgr. Carmelo Bajada, Bishop Nikol Cauch, Apostolic Nunzio, G. Maioli, and Archpriest Ġużeppi Grech on the day of the blessing of the cross

As the dome was rapidly closing, and the circles were getting smaller and smaller, expectations rose to a feverish pitch. Bets were being made that the dome and the lantern would be finished before the feast of the Baptist in June.

Several intrepid children were precariously climbing from the outside up on the dome, to see the progress for themselves and try to figure out how much work was left to finish it.

It was naturally after school hours when the workers had already left and gone for the day; archpriest Grech and the workers would not dare allow us to go anywhere near. However, somehow several managed to squeeze in. One had to climb steeply using heavy ladders, which old ladders were tied together with ropes so as to reach the desired level.

It is small wonder then that one fine day, as the writer was in pursuit of his friend Ġanni Xuereb *tal-Pikolin,* found himself utterly frozen with fear, barely hanging in the middle of a broken wooden ladder with missing rungs. Ġanni, quick as a wink, was already on top of the dome with the other children, some of whom could climb bare walls.

It was not a question of vertigo; this was incredibly dangerous. *Iċ-Ċens* menacingly hoves into view many storeys down below. Trembling and perspiring with unbelievable fear, this was the last time the writer "inspected" the dome.

The dome took twenty-two months to finish. It included the upper lantern with sixteen small windows.

The lantern is 12.1 meters (22 feet) high and has a diameter of 6.6 meters (22 feet). It has 16 windows that measure 3.3 meters (11 feet) by 75 centimeters (2 feet 6 inches).

Master mason Vella's greatest feat was on 12 May 1970 when at a height of seventy-five meters (246 feet), he closed the high dome. Ġużepp had enough reason to praise the Lord as well as the Baptist, who during 14 years of hard work and sacrifice was able to complete the Rotunda successfully.

Undoubtedly, this was his crowning glory. Tears rolled up in his eyes as he hammered with pride the last stone in place. There is little doubt, that only a master mason of the caliber of Ġużepp Vella could have built such a monumental church in a relatively such a short period.

Thus, the Rotunda became the biggest church with the highest dome on the Maltese islands. Its dimensions are as follows:

Length:	64 meters	(210 feet)
Width:	43 meters	(141 feet)
Height of Dome:	75 meters	(246 feet)
Circumference of Dome:	85 meters	(278 feet)
Internal Diameter:	25 meters	(82 feet)
External Diameter:	28 meters	(92 feet)

According to Simon Gaul, author of the Cadogan Island Guide, the Rotunda has the second highest dome, internally, in Europe. The Xewkija Dome comes second after the Vatican in Rome. It is six meters (20 feet) higher than St. Paul's Cathedral, in London. CNN points out that the Rotunda is the world's third highest unsupported dome.

Nineteen days later, on 31 May 1970, a cross measuring 2.5 meters (8.2 feet) by 2 meters (6.5feet) and weighing 72 kilos (159 pounds) was blessed by his Excellency Mons. G. Majoli, and placed in a two-ton cement block on top of the lantern.

The Apostolic Nunzio, G.Maioli, was chauffeured in a gorgeous 1969 red crimson convertible, Ford Thunderbird, driven by Lorry Spiteri *tal-Pixx*, as hundreds of people clapped on both sides.

Petards were let off. Church bells pealed joyfully while the *Prekursor* band marched on triumphantly to celebrate this undisputed, memorable occasion.

For archpriest Grech this was unmistakably the happiest and most wonderful day of his life; indeed this was the culmination of an incredible dream come true.

In a repeat of the blessing of the "First Stone" eighteen years before, the main square of Xewkija, was again choked with people from all over Gozo. This time, to celebrate and witness the happy hoisting of the cross on the lantern.

It was mainly due to archpriest Grech's unstinting efforts and ingenuity that such a daunting undertaking was finished in eighteen years, without respite. The *'tad-deffun'* and 'half-penny' critics who had brazenly avoided the village perspective were now speechless. They were nowhere to be seen.

With the most beatific, cheerful smile on his face, archpriest Grech delivered a passionate message to the faithful gathered in front of him that jammed and packed the central square; this was his great day.

He who for 18 years labored day and night to see his dream come to its fruition. He who was pitted against overwhelming odds spending many a sleepless night worrying over one hundred and one things was now incredibly officiating the blessing of the cross on the lantern of one of the largest domes in Christendom.

Here is an excerpt of his speech on this magical and wonderful occasion:

"On this most solemn, and important day, for the clergy and for the people of Xewkija, how blessed we feel, that right now we are surrounded by the Ecclesiastical and Civil Authorities of Malta and Gozo who are here with us. From the bottom of our hearts, we all raise towards heaven, a Hymn of Thanksgiving to God, for the great blessing He bestowed on us, that we are witnessing this monumental and colossal church built in honor of our great Precursor of Christ, our Patron St. John the Baptist.

> *I am personally most grateful to God for the special grace He gave me for being so resourceful, for the Clergy and the generosity of the people of Xewkija. I feel fortunate that in my lifetime I have seen this majestic Temple materialize from beginning to end.*
>
> *This is all the fruit of the patriotic and holy love that the people of Xewkija have for their land of birth and their Patron St. John the Baptist. One can say that a Temple of such grandeur was built with great laborious zeal and the money of the Xewkin, who live in the village and overseas.*

The lantern almost complete

May this enthusiasm, this fervor, and immense love, remain a light in our hearts, and the hearts of our children as in that of our forefathers, who left this noble and dear inheritance of patriotism from one generation to another, and who today from the tombs where they are resting, make their voices heard, so that with us they can celebrate and sing to God 'Te Deum Laudamus'.

Praise the Lord, that after 18 and a half years of continuous work, so many sacrifices and difficulties, today, amidst the happiness of our people, we are witnessing our wish and that of our forefathers finished and completed; that is to see the blessing and the placing of the Cross on this majestic and imposing dome of this grand and artistic Temple that is the joy of the Xewkin, the honor of Malta and Gozo and the admiration of tourists, who from every corner of the world visit and observe with great interest."

I would like to thank, the late but never forgotten Engineer and Designer, Mr. Ġuże' D'Amato, who sketched the plans in the style of a 'Croce Greca' and worked unstintingly without any remuneration, Architect Joe Mizzi who continued, without pay, the work of Mr. Ġuże', the late Chevalier Lorenzo Zammit Haber, who always assisted the architects and worked unflinchingly in all the tasks involving the old church and the new one, senza interessi.

I would also like, to thank the master masons of great skill Ġużepp Cauchi, and Toni Vella, who worked in the church for the first four and a half years; I wish to thank all the laborers who toiled from their hearts on this building. Special thanks go to master mason Ġużepp Vella, present here today. This resourceful master mason of great skill, during these last 14 continuous years built this imposing monument with great intellect, wisdom, and the utmost exactness. I also have the pleasure to say that these master stone masons and all the workers who all gave their share in one way or another regarding the construction of our edifice are all Xewkin Patriots.

Last but not least I would like to thank all those benefactors who gave their utmost to see this holy deed materialize

... this extraordinary feast will always be remembered, and its memory will remain forever registered amongst the most glorious episodes of Xewkija".

Seventeen months later, archpriest Grech was waiting to board the ferry in Mġarr harbor to cross over to Malta and order the German clear glass panes for the windows of the dome. Suddenly and without warning, a truck going downhill loaded with empty gas cylinders lost its brakes and careened into a wall.

One of the cylinders that flew on impact regrettably hit archpriest Grech on the head. As a consequence of this harrowing accident, after four days in a coma, he passed away, on 18 October 1971. Archpriest Grech was sixty-three years old.

His funeral made up of a huge cortege started from Mġarr harbor and proceeded slowly, followed by hundreds of people. All of Xewkija came to say goodbye.

As he had correctly predicted twenty-three years earlier, archpriest Grech died a martyr for Xewkija. His venerable wish was prophetically fulfilled. *"There is no greater love than to lay down one's life for one's friends"*. John 15-13

Without fanfare, archpriest Grech threw himself wholeheartedly to oversee the building of a monumental church while serving the spiritual and the physical needs of the poor. He lost no time redeeming the poor and the downtrodden, secretly offering them enough money and encouragement to get by with their harsh lives.

Archpriest Grech was pious, zealous and pure of heart. He worked unceasingly for the spiritual good of the people. He was charitable and humble and had a great devotion to the Blessed Sacrament; he would regularly spend time in prayer at the foot of the altar.

The writer remembers an anecdote that Mgr. Ġwann Azzopardi, the curator at the Cathedral Museum in Mdina, recounted during lunch held at Bacchus restaurant in honor of Victor Pasmore's 80th birthday.

Toni with his Dodge workhorse

Ta' Randu supplied most of the stones until the very end, many a times at a special, discounted price.

Courtesy
Randu Zammit

102 - The Rotunda

It was when archpriest Grech had invited him to give the Lenten sermons to the female teenagers of the village of Xewkija. He (archpriest Grech) had told him to admonish these young girls with fire and brimstone if they ever dared to wear the newly introduced miniskirts of that era.

Every week without exception, archpriest Grech would venture to the merchant shops in Rabat to verify and confirm that there were no outstanding bills regarding any item or material procured in connection with the construction of the church. He totally abhorred any form of debt.

Archpriest Grech will always be remembered with reverence and gratitude. After affectionately baptizing hundreds of children, including the writer, we all felt orphans upon the sudden tragic death of our brave but shy and much-beloved archpriest. One and all deeply lamented him.

And everyone cried.

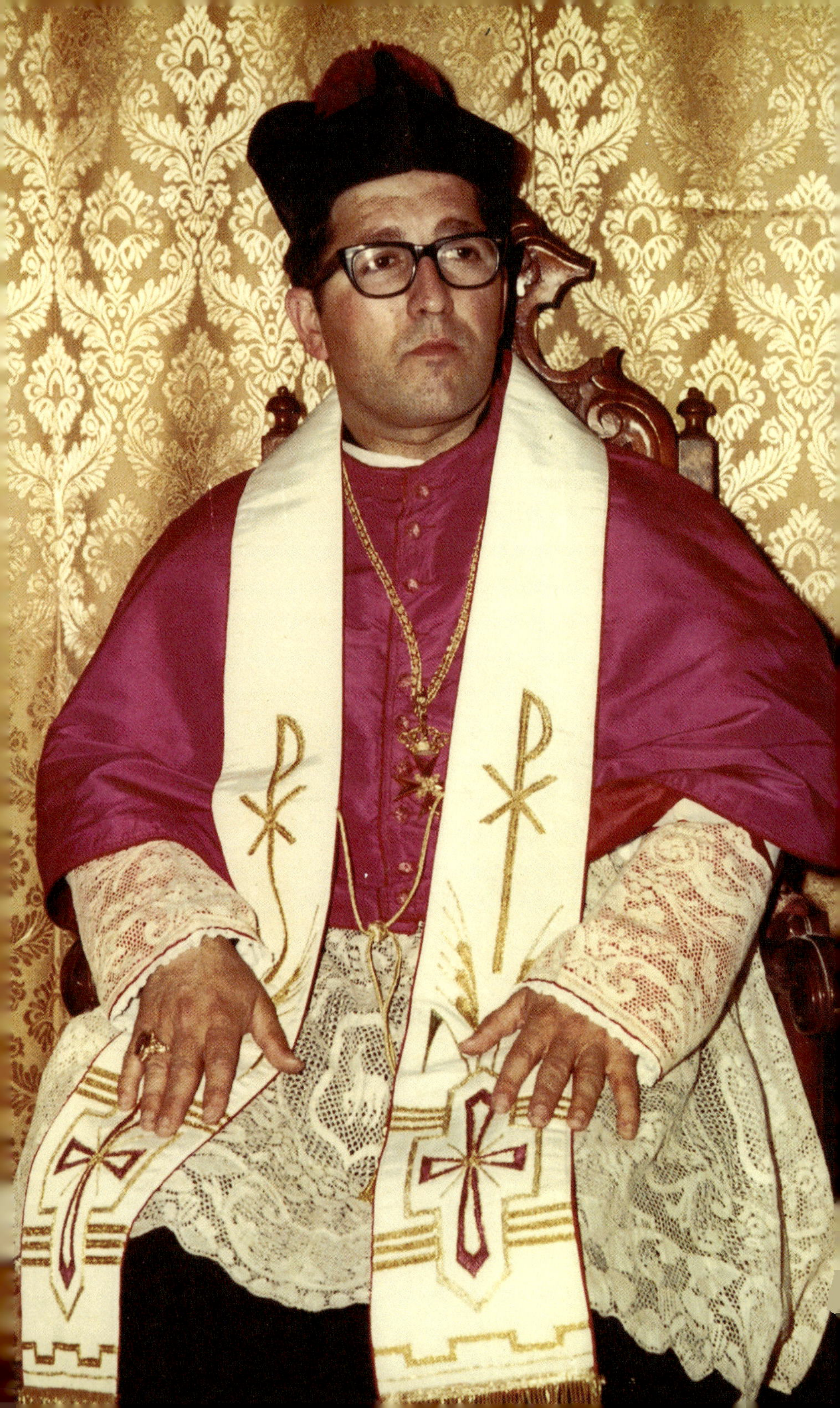

Chapter Eight

Beyond The Rotunda

Yet time will prove where wisdom lies.
Matthew 11:16-19

Although you have never seen him, you love him, and without seeing him, you now believe in him and rejoice with inexpressible joy touched with glory because you are achieving faith's goal, your salvation.
From the first letter of Peter 1:3-9

The sudden, tragic death of archpriest Grech left the entire village of Xewkija in tears. It was a huge loss. Such a deep void rendered the people speechless.

The old church was still standing and although the cross crowned the dome, an enormous amount of work still needed to be done.

It included the difficult and dangerous work of dismantling the precious carved stone 'lacework' and installing it in the new museum. The question, therefore, of who was going to succeed archpriest Grech, became one of paramount importance.

In consultation with a special committee formed for this purpose, the Clergy agreed on one clergyman: Dun Karm Mercieca. This request was presented to the new Bishop Nikol Cauchi in no uncertain terms.

This was not a threat but a promise. After deliberating for three months, on 18 January 1972, Dun Karm Mercieca *tal-Gardell*, was confirmed archpriest of Xewkija.

The news was edifying for the people of Xewkija, and indeed the whole village was elated and for good reason. Dun Karm was born in Xewkija but grew up in Rabat, in the shadows of the Basilica of St. George. For some time, he served as its assistant pastor.

Archpriest Carmelo Mercieca

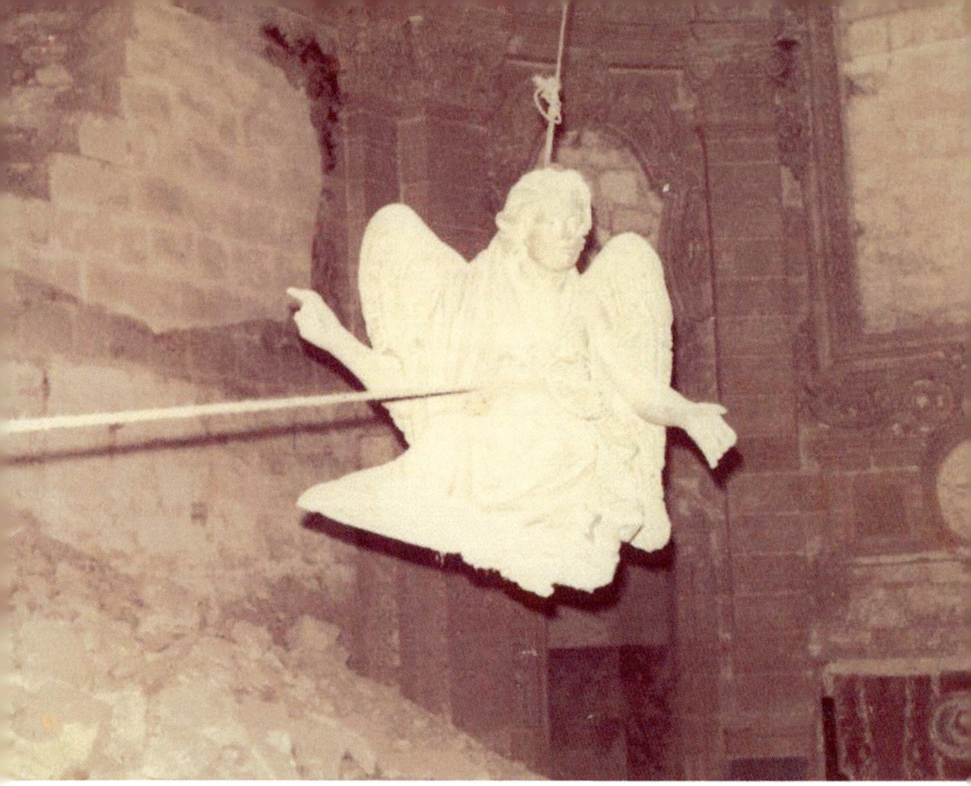

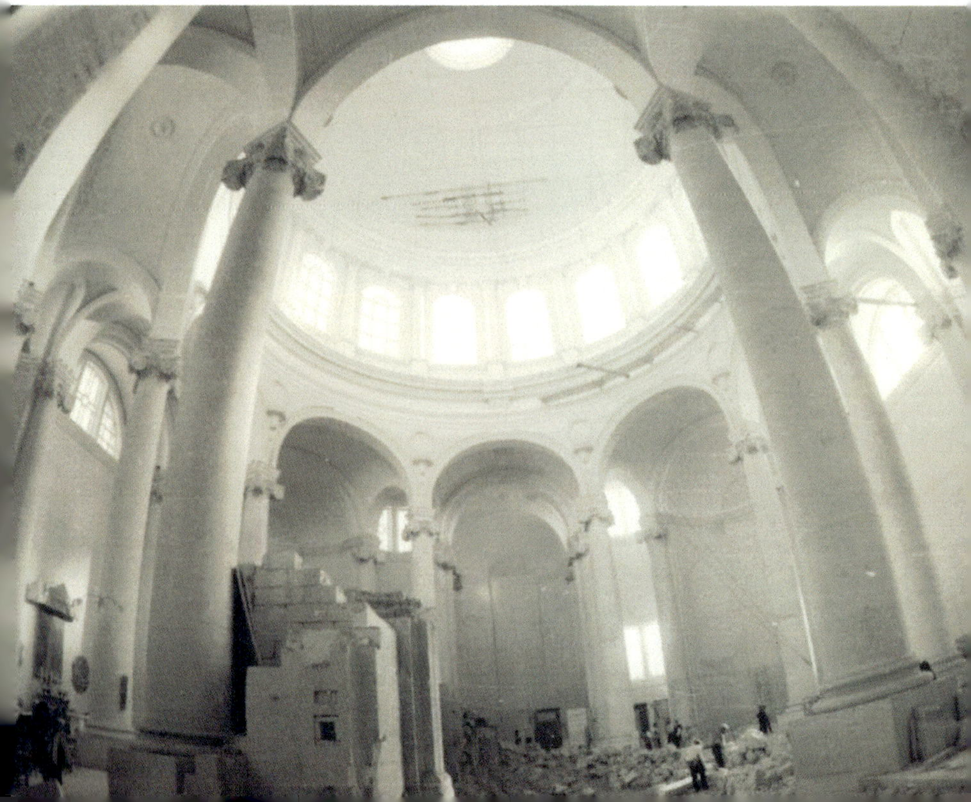

Later, Dun Karm was one of the Spiritual Directors of Oratorju Don Bosco, the biggest youth institution in Gozo that also hosted a wide-screen cinema.

Unlike his predecessor, Dun Karm was outgoing, highly experienced and had a substantial appreciation and understanding of literature, arts, and music. His forte was undoubtedly the theater. Immensely popular with the youths of Rabat Dun Karm was sincerely and deeply missed when he eventually left.

Dun Karm was chosen to work in various Curia Commissions, amongst which he served as Secretary of the Catechetical Commission.

There is no doubt that Dun Karm had all the requisite qualities for the village of Xewkija, which sadly, at that time, was still lacking, particularly when it pertained to cultural and social activities. Many were those half-taught and half-asleep.

An angel coming down to earth

The vacancy was now filled. An expert in holding meetings and activities for various groups that hailed from any sector of society, Dun Karm, barely 31 years old was full of energy. He grabbed every opportunity for the betterment and advancement of his parishioners.

Archpriest Mercieca had an enormous advantage: he had the full backing of his numerous, close-knit, erudite family, which included a priest, Dun Ġorġ and his brother Bennie, a Museum Superior.

It marked a huge difference as there was no question that whenever he needed something, the newly appointed archpriest knew that he could rely on the support and advice that was being proffered to him.

The writer vividly remembers archpriest Mercieca pulling his cassock up to his waist, grabbing a shovel to help the volunteers. They were mixing cement in a Benford to lay the concrete floor for the internal paving of the new church.

Those standing there were awestruck. Many were put to shame by his genuine eagerness and passionate enthusiasm. We were not used to this. In fact, we never expected or imagined that our new archpriest would do manual work.

Ganmaria's Caterpillar bulldozer was used to clear the rubble inside the new church

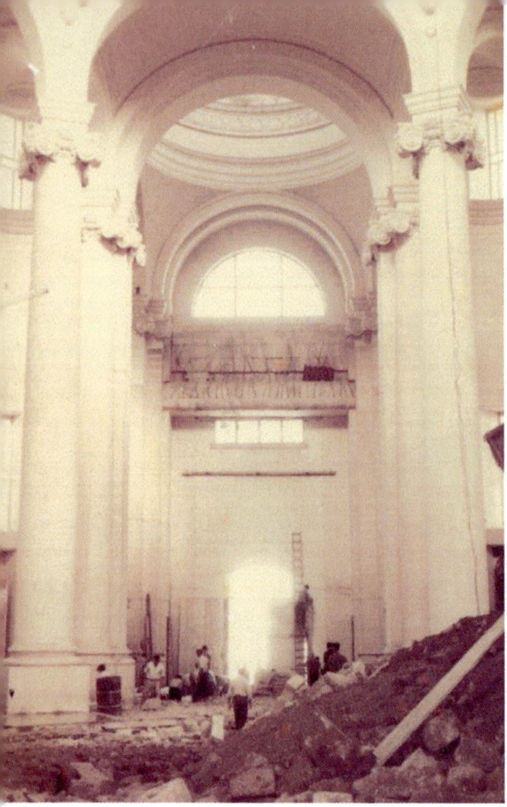
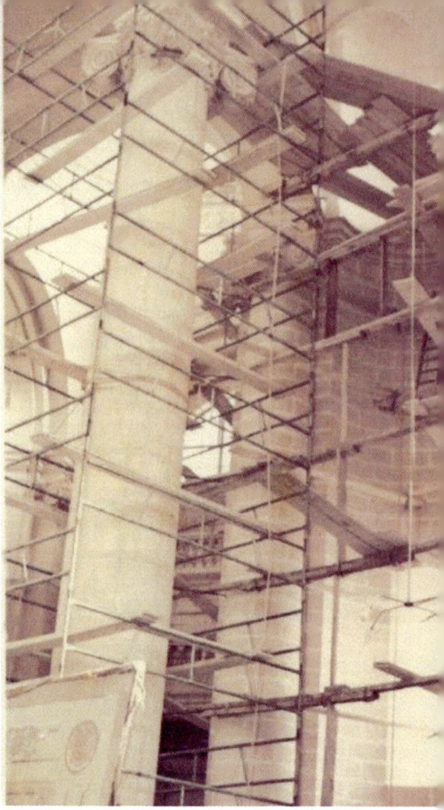
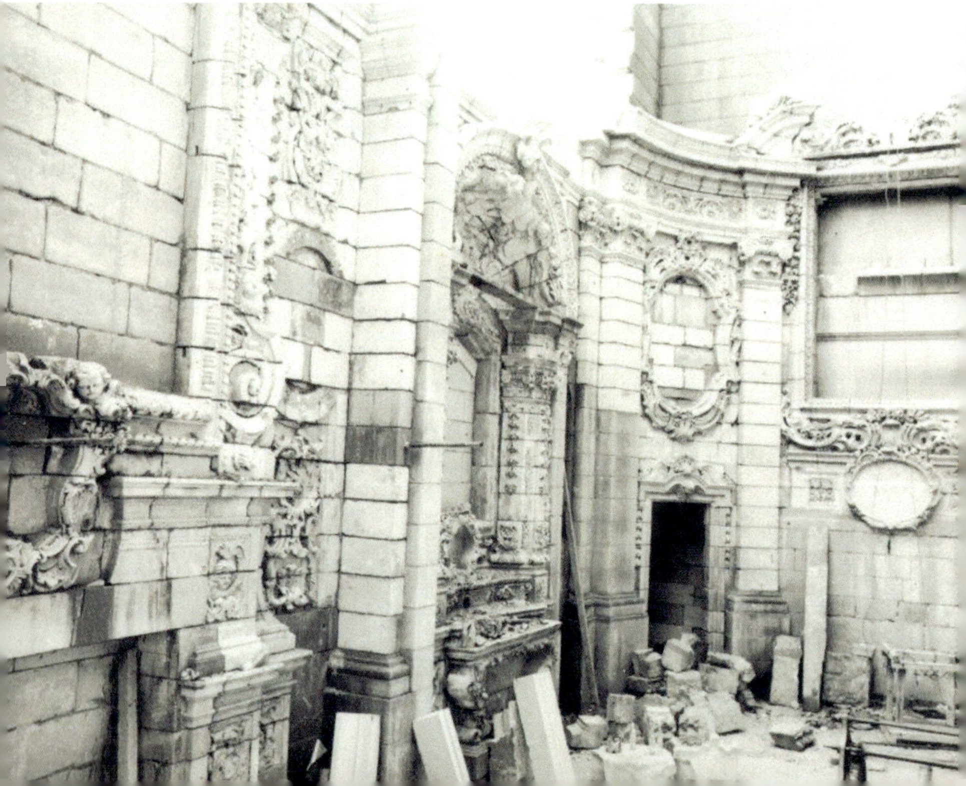

We thought that construction work was for laborers only. However, Dun Karm was not afraid to dirty his hands and willingly would join the workers in whatever task was necessary to see that work was accomplished efficiently. This example took root and now one and all pitched in.

In less than a fortnight, archpriest Mercieca mesmerized and stupefied the whole village, both with his words that were golden, as well as by his strong-willed determination and example.

Tons of rubble was cleared from the old church

His inspiration was a clear direction and a shining characteristic worthy of imitation; it was a call to all those concerned who had cast their doubts.

Archpriest Mercieca's strategy was primarily two-pronged: to finish the new church so that parishioners would have an excellent service in a decent church; and secondly, the Pastoral Organization of the Parish itself.

In the end modern scaffolding was used

Single handedly he mobilized the village to clear the old church, so that on 2 April 1972, the last mass was said on the major altar of the old church.

It was evident that Xewkija gained an undisputed teacher and an unyielding leader. He knew and readily understood the great difficulties that lay ahead, but nevertheless, he was now committed to resolving them as best he could. For him, nothing was insurmountable.

Dun Karm made it a point that every single individual could and should contribute something. Moreover, by this he was not just referring to a monetary donation. He wanted all youths to be seriously involved.

It was crucial psychologically for many youths because by being involved one felt that they were making a valid contribution, and so naturally, everyone became aware and more conscious of his or her self-esteem. Self-confidence shot up as a consequence.

The difficult building of the Museum of Sculpture by Toni Camilleri

All youths were urged to interact and participate actively while hearing mass. In church, if one did not read the first lesson as a catechist, then one was supposed to do the collection. Alternatively, sing or play an instrument: the piano, an organ or a guitar.

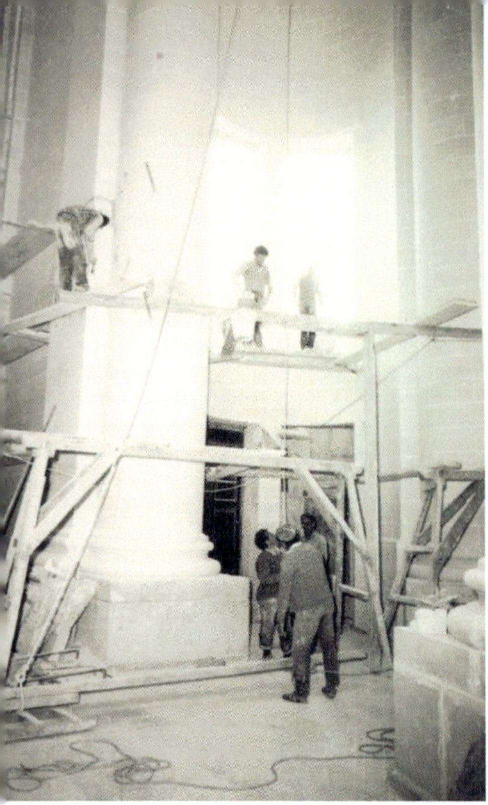

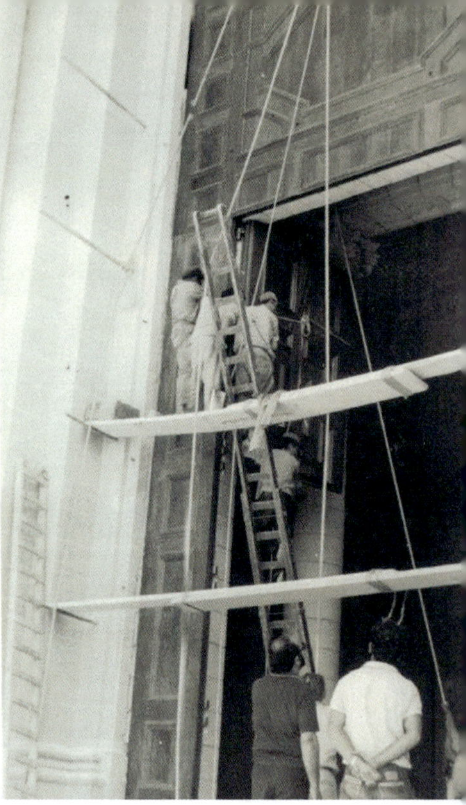

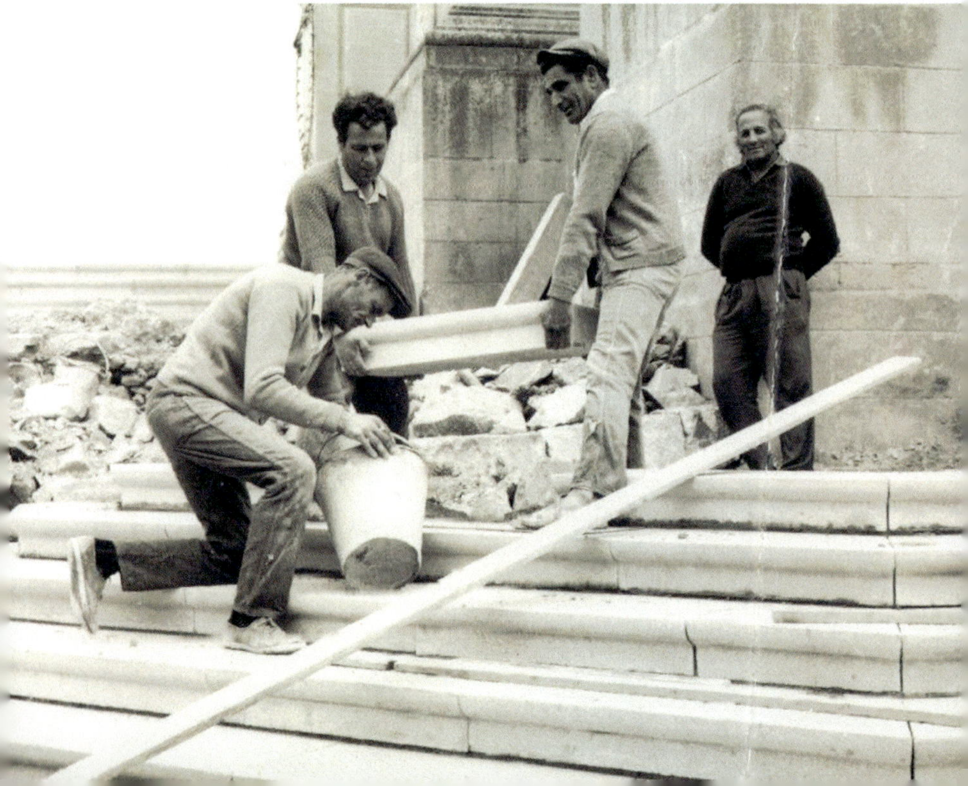

For Dun Karm correctly believed that everyone has a talent and by actively involving youths, the mentality of the *Xewkin* was changed practically overnight.

He immediately transmitted a sense of purpose, a sense of hope. A brilliant orator, Mercieca spoke with such fervor and eloquence that left his parishioners spellbound. His four-door sedan, a small, gray Isuzu Gemini car, became a sort of mini-bus, giving rides to one and all.

A Choir, *Vox Clamantis*, was established and a dramatic circle, *Għaqda Drammatika* Xewkija, was formed. Today it is known as *Teatru Ġiovanni*.

The first production was a light opera, *Fior di Loto*. Many other such productions followed, regaling hundreds of theater lovers from across the island.

It was an exceedingly positive influence on our upbringing. Interaction between young males and females was no longer taboo but encouraged.

Back to the building of the church. Żakkarija and his young crew included a couple of his able sons, Ġużepp, and Salvu. They started the arduous and perilous work of carefully pointing with trowels and sanding with cock's comb and sandpaper the internal dome from top to bottom.

The last finishing touch meant that every single stone, every single crevice had to be expertly pointed and sanded finely by hand. Then, on 9 January 1973, another tragedy struck. Salvu Azzopardi *ta' Ċellu*, one of the young workers pointing high up in the dome, for some reason, lost his balance and fell to his death. He was seventeen.

The writer, a distant relative of the victim, sat next to Salvu in the classroom in the primary school. He had a collection of little green fern leaves.

Occasionally Salvu would give the writer a leaf or two to place neatly between the pages of the school book. Salvu, like many other youngsters before him, adamantly refused to continue his education and instead opted to drop out and start work at the first opportunity that came by.

Workers pointing and finely sanding down, stone by stone, crevice by crevice the new church

Salvu Tabone and workers installing the six tons teak door, measuring 10 by 4.8 meters (33 x 16 feet).

Toni Camilleri, foreground, laying the new parvis

Manuel (Leli) Saliba, from Għarb, chief stone builder of the beautiful perspectives

Ġuże' Galea, from Rabat, Malta, designed the beautiful geometric marble floor, the splendid perspectives and revised the plans and sketches of the belfry tower so as to be in proportion of the dome.

112 - The Rotunda

One can imagine the feelings of dismay and sadness of the community. Everyone was numb. He was given a funeral befitting a true hero of Xewkija. There is no doubt that Salvu will remain so, forever. Archpriest Mercieca had to suffer and endure a cruel twist of fate; it was to be his baptism of fire.

In the words of Carl Gustav Jung: *"There are as many nights as days, and the one is just as long as the other in the year's course. Even a happy life cannot be without a measure of darkness, and the word 'happy' would lose its meaning if it were not balanced by sadness."*

A photo of Salvu, together with that of Pawlu Vella, is today placed next to each other in the vestry underneath the portraits of all the Parish Priests that faithfully served this beloved village.

In March 1973, the first pageant of Our Lady of Sorrows was held. *Id-Duluri* turned out to be an enormous success since it was the only live pageant to be held a week before the Passion procession of Good Friday.

Natural wariness eased into friendliness. Bit by bit, the entire village of Xewkija was transformed; it was never the same again. The whole village progressed forward by quantum leaps. If anything, Dun Karm will long be remembered as 'the great reformer.'

The writer remembers Emmanuel Gatt *ta' Ġanmaria*, from Rabat, whose wife is from Xewkija, bulldozing the debris left from the old church, partly *pro bono*, with his old but powerful Caterpillar.

One of the first dozen battered trucks that volunteered to line up for the clearing of the rubble was a Bedford belonging to Pawlu Agius *tal-Passalun*. Pawlu, like many others, always did his level best to help out, and when he could not drive his truck, he invariably sent one of his sons.

The days of the mule and donkey carts and pulleys and wicker baskets were, thankfully, history. Bulldozers and heavy machinery were now the order of the day.

The work involved was difficult and sometimes dangerous

On 29 August 1973, Bishop Mons., Nikol Cauchi placed and solemnly blessed the first stone of the Museum of Sculpture.

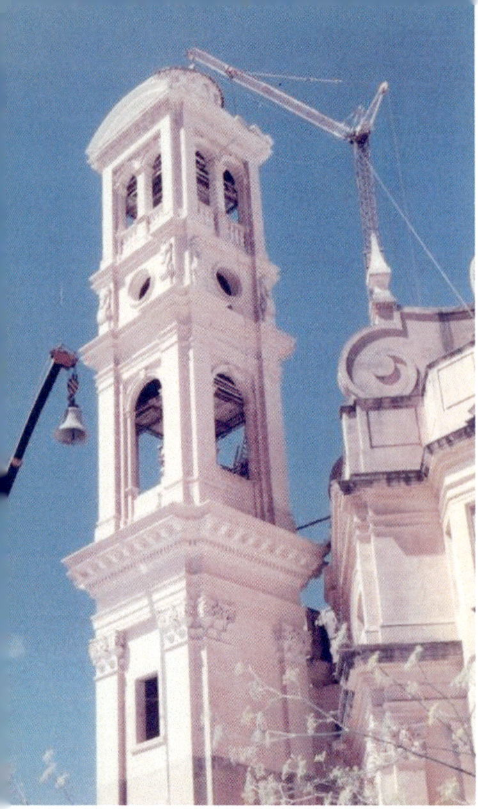

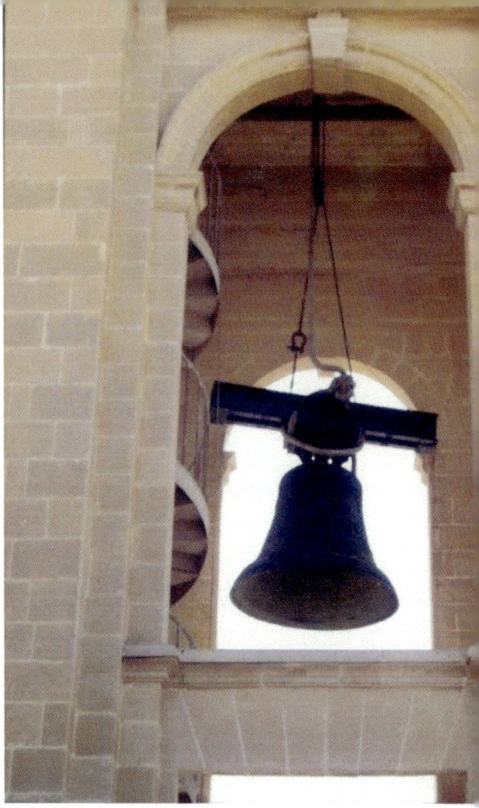

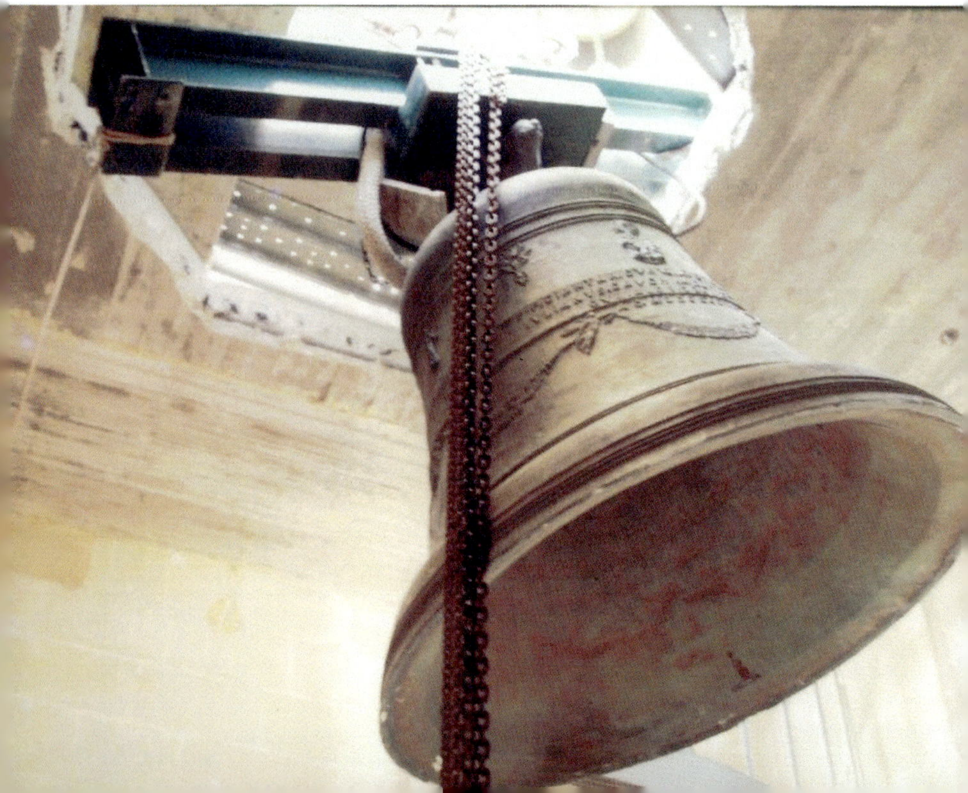

Heavy machinery including big cranes were used for the building of the belfry tower and the hoisting of the new bells

One of the new bells on its way up

Another bell from John Taylor Bell founders, of Loughborough, U.K., the largest bell foundry in the world.

Courtesy Parish Archive

The large iron door keys of the old church were placed in this stone together with coins and a parchment to record this occasion. Toni Camilleri took charge of this difficult and hazardous task. Toni did a magnificent job. He was ably assisted by Żakkarija Cilia, Ġużepp Pace *ta' Pawla*, and several other expert laborers.

They painstakingly dismantled the rich Rococo interior of the old church, stone by stone, like "Lego". These stones of exquisite refinement and linearity date back to 1665. These amazing stones include motifs such as angels, shells, scrolls, branches and flowers, all in delicate and ingenious compositions.

Photographing and carefully numbering each and every exceptional stone, Toni rebuilt it delicately, exactly the same way as it was before and placed it in the new annex.

When it came to building the complicated recess, Toni Camilleri requested the expert assistance of master mason Ġużepp Vella, who duly obliged. On a side note, master mason Vella was commissioned to finish the beautiful church of Tarxien, in Malta. Once inside this church, the keen observer will notice the real genius of this master mason as nowhere is the magic and brilliance of the Maltese stone so manifest and distinctly well built.

The fascinating iconography and symbols of the old sepulchral slabs of the tombstones that were dug up from the old church were now laid once again in the Museum of Sculpture.

Among these slabs, one finds that of *Kappillan* (archpriest) Pietro Aquilina and that of the Zammit Haber family. Generosity is a reason for gratitude and joy. This time-consuming, meticulous work was finished and blessed by Bishop Nikol Cauchi on 18 June 1974. Today, the dignity and simplicity of this museum is a real masterpiece and a special attraction for tourists to view and appreciate. Entrance to this museum is free.

In the meantime, mass was now said at an improvised side chapel on the left-hand side of the new church until all works were finished. It included the proper leveling of the massive internal ground, which entailed and called for another round of tremendous work and the pouring of yards and yards of concrete.

Meanwhile, Nisju Tabone together with the constant help of his brother Manwel Tabone *id-Demusi*, and other volunteers installed the sixteen clear-glass windows underneath the dome. Nisju ingeniously made an elegant master-frame form using zinc; he would fill the form with concrete and iron, and then place and fit it exactly in the window. All the window frames came out to near perfection.

In the meantime, a warehouse was built on Racecourse Street, to store all the objects such as lights, banners and decorations that are used for the religious feast, including the scaffolding.

Another important work was being carried out in the front elevation and the façade, the various shells, the transepts, the choir, and all the niches. This called for great skill and scrupulous work by many an able *Xewki*, who after work and particularly on Sundays and Public Holidays, would go with mallet and chisel in hand, to perform this arduous task.

So that on 15 June 1973, the Rotunda was blessed and officially opened by the Bishop of Gozo, Mons. N.G. Cauchi. It was to be the first titular feast celebrated in the new church.

For this occasion the Bishops of Malta, Mons. Archbishop Mikiel Gonzi, Mons. Bishop Emmanuel Galea and Mons E. M. Gerada were all present. The Apostolic Nunzio Mons Edoardo Pecoraio accompanied them.

Now the open space inside the new structure was big and airy. Now the time of fighting to grab a chair in the cramped, tired, dark space of the old church was happily a thing of the past. The villagers wanted such a church, and now they gasped at its mighty, opulent interior. The beauty, as well as the magnificent display of the sculpted Gozitan limestone, is nowhere so apparent in these islands.

An appeal was made directly to families to contribute for the new wooden pews required in the church that were to be far more comfortable to kneel or sit on. Incredibly, within two months, the necessary funds were all pledged, and the chairs that encumbered the church were promptly removed.

A year later, the six tons main door, measuring 10 meters (33 feet) by 4.8 meters (16 feet) was carried out and installed by Salvu Tabone *ta' Gurġuna*. He was assisted, by Toni Camilleri. The door is made of teak on the exigent design of Anton Saliba, from Rabat. It was paid entirely by the Pace brothers *tal-Bubus*.

Toni Camilleri did a new '*Bankun*'. Inside this large bench, Emmanuel Attard *ta' Fantin* expertly welded an array of steel drawers and compartments where to store sacred vestments.

Next in line was the enormous parvis in front of the Rotunda, also laid by Toni Camilleri. The hall on top of the sacristy was now finished, and Bishop Cauchi blessed the marble Major Altar, executed by the Italian firm Cecotti. The reputable Gozitan firm, A.F. Ellis, laid the marble presbytery. Meanwhile the installation of an elaborate electrical system, designed by engineer Albert Camilleri, was carried out by Joseph Hili and his company Hilite, of Xewkija.

In May 1978, archpriest Mercieca was elevated to Honorary Monsignor of the Cathedral Chapter. A month later, in June 1978, the Rotunda church was consecrated by Roman Cardinal Silvio Oddi. Local bishops participated in this solemn tercentennial feast. These were His Grace, Mgr. Michael Gonzi, Archbishop Emeritus, and Archbishop Ġużeppi Mercieca of Malta, Nunzio Apostolic Antonio del Giudice, and Bishop Mons., Nikol Cauchi of Gozo.

The Archbishop felt that the Third Centenary celebrations would be a splendid opportunity to choose the Xewkija Parish Church as the Spiritual Seat of the Sovereign Military Order of St. John in Gozo.

The idea was accepted by the members of the Association's Council. It also had the seal of approval of His Eminence the Prince and Grand Master of the Order, Fra Angelo de Mojana di Cologna.

The sacred relic of the Hand of St. John the Baptist was kindly lent to Xewkija for the occasion by the Patriarch of Venice, Cardinal Albino Luciani, later, Pope John Paul I.

Another relic, the hand which baptized Jesus, is said to have great miraculous powers. Sultan Baiazet donated

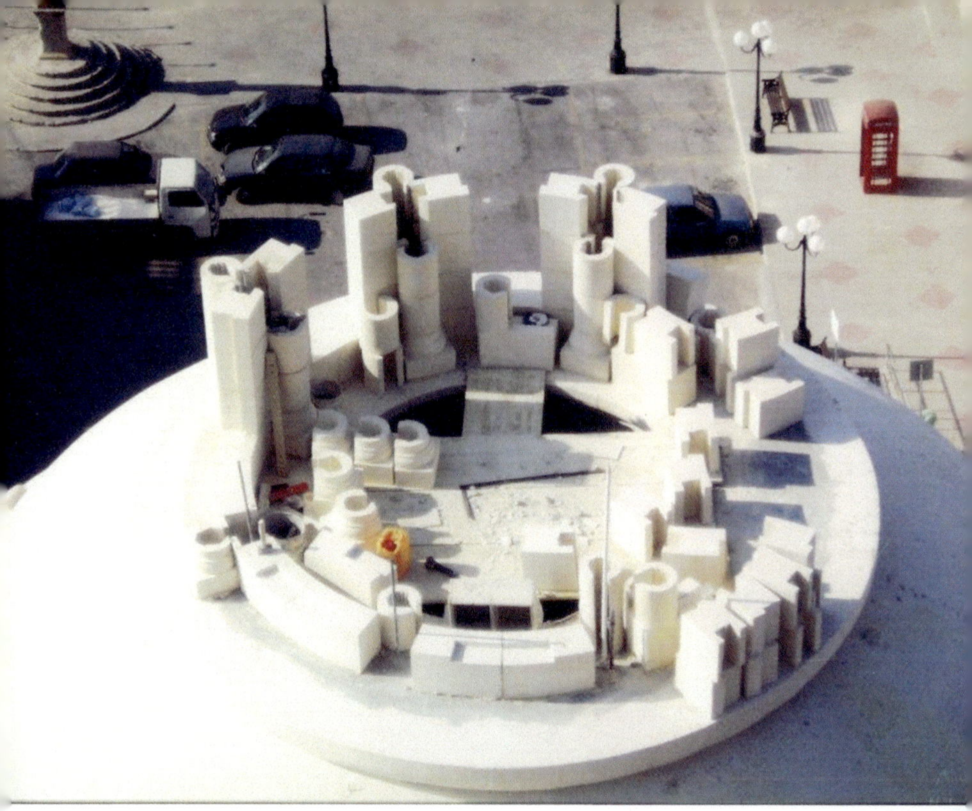

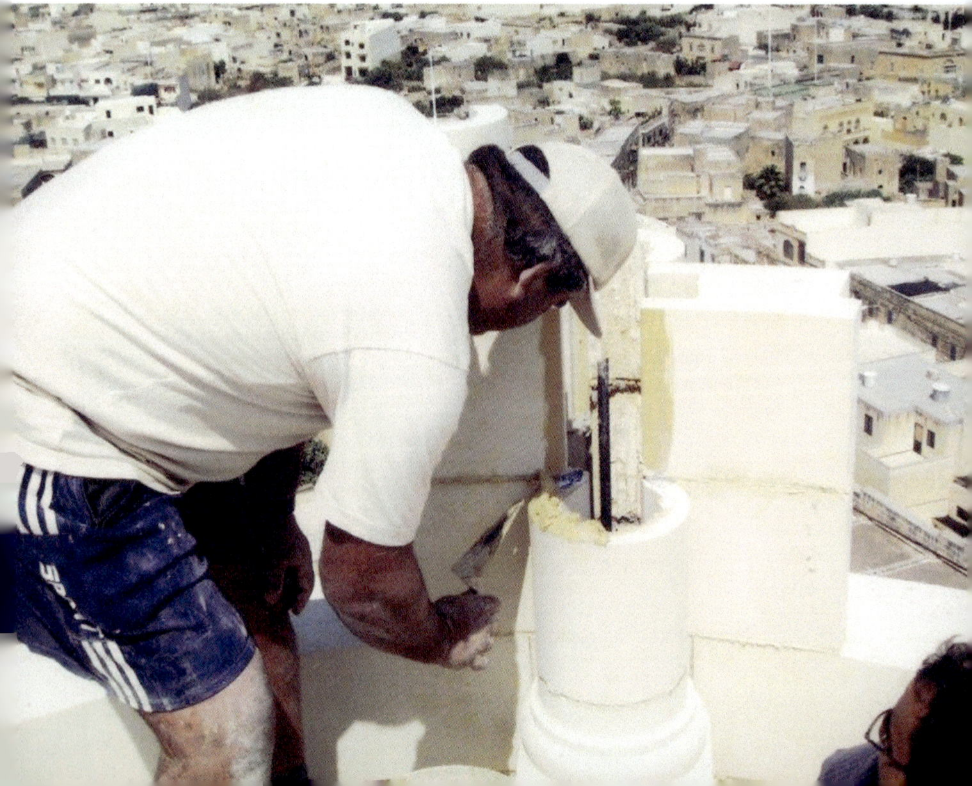

it to Grand Master d'Aubusson in 1484. The first and last German Grand Master Ferdinand von Hompesch took it with him to Ljubljana, Slovenia, in 1798, as he fled Malta on the arrival of Napoleon Bonaparte and his Republican troops.

The reliquary loaned by the Patriarch of Venice was brought over safely in a precious sphere made of gold and exquisite stones by the writer's brother then a newly ordained priest, Dun Ġwann Mizzi. Dun Ġwann Attard accompanied him. Together they spirited their way clandestinely, first on foot over the Rialto bridge through the thick crowds of medieval Venice, and then by boat, train, and plane like two secret agents in disguise.

The empty monstrance for the relic of St. John the Baptist is today found at St. John's Co-Cathedral in Valletta. During the 17th century, this relic was carried in a procession on the feast of St. John the Baptist, with fervent veneration and much pomp.

The Rotunda now had a semblance of a beautiful princess, but a princess with no shoes, nonetheless. So with immense vigor, archpriest Mercieca set about his work to tap funds from overseas. The indefatigable archpriest duly left for Australia, where there is a large community of *Xewkin*.

Archpriest Mercieca was greatly assisted by Frenċ Saliba, *ta' Kuzzu* in Sydney and by Salvu Haber in Melbourne. Two perspectives are dedicated to these emigrants. Shortly afterward, this appeal was launched by another trip to North America, this time, to two major cities, New York and later, Toronto.

On account of this, the *Xewkin* emigrants, who never relinquished their veneration for St. John the Baptist, were very generous and gave wholeheartedly.

Thus, the money was successfully raised to continue the work. The late Mgr. Carmelo Bajada handled all the paperwork for the overseas bank transfers of the sums collected.

Once again, the respected firm A.F.Ellis clinched the substantial contract to lay the expensive Carrara marble flooring. The marble was sourced from the same quarries

The lantern of the cupola under construction

Chief Mason Raymond Vella finishing the lantern of the Cupola

Courtesy Parish Archive

that provided Michelangelo with the marble for his statue of 'David'.

This beautiful geometric marble floor was laid on the design of Ġuże' Galea, from Rabat, Malta. However, the marble itself was laid under the expert supervision of Toni Saliba, *ta' Komu*, from Rabat, a marmista of exceptional skills. The marble consisted of Arabesco, Botticino, Rossa Alicante and Rossa Sant'Agata.

Again, Ġuże' Galea rose to the occasion to design the beautiful perspectives. This work, carried out in a decorative style, was superbly executed by the chief stone builder, Manuel (*Leli*) Saliba, from Għarb.

The intricate and elaborate sculpture, including the columns of these perspectives by *tal-Gims* family, is easily discerned. It is all sculpted by Ġużepp and his brother Kristinu Camilleri.

The old parish house in the square was pulled down. Instead, an elegant three storey edifice on the design of Perit Joseph P. Dimech went up to accommodate the Parochial Centre.

It became the main venue for *Teatru Ġiovanni*, where various stage plays and cultural events are held every year. It also hosts *Radju Prekursur*, the brainchild of Mr. Frans Galea.

Under the supervision of the renowned Perit Alex Torpiano, chief builder Toni Axiaq *ta' Rafel ta' Xanaħ*, from Żebbuġ, started the building of the splendid eastern belfry tower. The design was by expert Ġuże' Galea.

Master mason Ġuzepp Vella ceremoniously laid the first stone. It was blessed by Mgr., Bishop Nikol Cauchi, on Monday 15 June 1987. (But this stone is actually of the western belfry that has yet to be built).

This time there was no need for wooden poles and pulleys or winches. A huge crane was set up to hoist all the stone and material, including the concrete that was supplied and provided in appropriate ready mix trucks.

Three years later, the remarkable eastern campanile rising to an incredible height of 56.3 meters (185 feet) was finished. It was blessed by Bishop Cauchi on 29 August 1991 on the occasion of the Feast of the Beheading of St. John the Baptist and accompanied by marches played by the *Prekursur* band. A group of volunteers did all the pointing in their spare time.

Since June 2006, this beautiful bell tower houses three new bells that were brought over from John Taylor Bell Founders, of Loughborough, U.K. According to campanologist, Kenneth Cauchi, John Taylor is the largest bell foundry in the world.

Another considerable sum of money, close to 300,000 euro, was collected to procure these fine bells. The largest bell, Giovanna, has a diameter of 2050 mm; (six feet seven inches) Eliżabetta has a diameter of 1435mm, (four feet seven inches) and Marija Addolorata has a diameter of 1080mm (three feet five inches).

Under the steady and expert direction of Toni Grima *ta' Ċappelli*, aided by several other volunteers, these enormous and heavy bells were successfully hoisted up and installed in the new campanile. Each bell took six hours to hoist up, using a 10-ton chain block.

Mikelanġ Sapiano's mechanical clock of 1875 found its new place in this bell tower. It is integrated with two of the old bells, one by Aloysius Bouchut of Valletta (1738) and the smaller one by Paccard of Annecy, France (1949).

In a fascinating article, Josmar Azzopardi describes in detail how Pullu Xerri from Xewkija, spent nineteen months *pro bono*, ingeniously restoring and incorporating the giant one-face clock to operate with four faces.

It meant changing the clock from a rudimental birdcage design to a flatbed design set in a *campanile* room measuring 6.4 meters by 6.4 meters (21 feet). It is quite an engineering feat in itself.

Pullu Xerri ensures, and the writer can confidently confirm, that the clock chimes precisely on the hour, every hour all year round.

It also tolls regularly and without exception, at every 15 minute interval and can be heard from just about every quarter of the village. Can. Adrian Gourgion must be pleased.

Aside from adding three beautiful bells, Dun Ġorġ Mercieca, who is also the assistant pastor, was instrumental, in installing a new sound system. This sophisticated system is equipped with the latest technology provided by Mr. Albert Van der Houf, at a cost of almost 10,000 euro.

The acoustics of the 3,000 seat capacity interior of the Rotunda are now deemed so perfect, that every sound can be heard with warmth and depth by the congregation.

Michael Vella Ltd expertly installed a modern hydraulic elevator that can take up a maximum of 13 persons or 1,000 kilos. At that time, it was the highest elevator on the islands.

For a small donation, visiting tourists can now easily and comfortably ride up the 21 meters (69 feet), and get a bird's eye view of the entire island. Once up there, one can examine up close the amazing dome and its sister cupola next to it; one can even climb higher up onto the bell tower itself, weather and vertigo permitting.

On the 22nd October 2004, the Rotunda church was chosen by Bishop Nikol Cauchi to host the Universalis Presbyterorum Conventus of the Congregatio Pro Clericis. This highly prestigious event was proudly convened. It was attended by clerics from all over the world, including numerous Cardinals, among which were:

Jean-Louis Tauran, Pontifical Archivist and Librarian, Vatican City; Cormac Murphy-O'Connor, Archbishop of Westminster, U.K., Georg Maximilian Sterzinsky, Archbishop of Berlin; Angelo Sodano of Venice; Julio Terrazas, Archbishop of Bombay, India; Sean Patrick O'Malley, Archbishop of Boston, USA; Marian Jaworsky, Archbishop of Lviv of Ukraine; Peter Kodwo Appiah Turkson, Archbishop of Cape Coast, Ghana; Francisco Alvarez Martinez, Archbishop Emeritus of Toledo, Spain, Crescenzio Sepe, Prefect of the Congregation for the Evangelization of Peoples, Vatican City; Juan Esquerda Bifet, Theologian, Spain; Raniero Cantalamessa, o.f.m., Preacher of the Papal Household, Italy.

The fine cupola on the entrance was proudly started by chief mason Raymond, Ġużepp Vella's youngest son, on 10 December 1994, under the direction of Perit Alex

Torpiano. Raymond was ably assisted on a voluntary basis by Toni Grima and a host of skilled laborers. It must have been a very moving experience and a high honor for the young mason Raymond.

There he could see and touch the passion of this building his late, dear father had merited with great honor into this sacred edifice.

The cupola was finished in March 2007, and the cross was placed on top of the new dome on 9 June 2007. Gozo Bishop Mario Grech blessed the cross and the new dome. The 62-kilo redwood cross, made by Ġanni Zammit *tar-Rest* was placed on top of it.

On this occasion Mgr. Grech led a solemn concelebration with the participation of the *Vox Clamantis* choir and the orchestra under the direction of his brother, maestro Carmel Grech. The lovely stone sculpture of the organ gallery is all the work of Toni Camilleri.

After the cross had been placed on top of the cupola, a barrage of fireworks and petards were let off. The Mayor of Xewkija, Dr. Monica Vella, in the presence of Archpriest Mgr. Karm Mercieca inaugurated the new lighting system for the dome.

This beautiful cupola is built on the same design of architect Ġuze' D'Amato. Chief mason Raymond Vella was assisted by his expert stone-cutters, Charles Azzopardi, Ġużepp Xerri *tal-Bokkli* while Raymond Farrugia, *taz-Zajzu* and Ġużepp Camilleri *tal-Gims* did all the stone sculpture.

The cupola measures 26.8metres (88 feet) in height and has a diameter of 10 meters (33 feet) from inside and 10.9metres (36 feet) from outside, respectively. It has eight galvanized windows designed and manufactured by Ġuzepp Attard *ta' Fantin*.

Meanwhile, intrepid veteran Ġużepp Pace single-handedly saw to the outside pointing of the whole cupola.

Ġużepp's brother, Ġanni *ta' Pawla*, was later eulogized at his funeral by Archpriest Mercieca as, *"a man who was worth the equal of 100 men"*.

This apt eulogy was for all the volunteer work that Ġanni had freely contributed towards the church and parish during his lifetime.

From inside, the pointing and sanding down were ably done by a dedicated group of volunteers led by Felix Vella, Ġużepp Cilia, Ġużepp Pace, brothers Ġanni and Mario Axiaq, and Paul Attard.

The concrete roof and the scaffolding were cleared away by Chalie Attard, Raymond Attard, Charlon Buttigieg, Pawlu Attard, Luke Galea, Jonathan Azzopardi, Charles Borg and Marjohn Hili.

It is with great pride that keen volunteers like these get a mention. Aside from the generous monetary contributions, it is genuine men like these who deserve great credit for getting such perilous works done.

One surely cannot forget Frenċ Farrugia *taz-Zajzu,* and Marjanu Pace *tal-Balakk*, among many others.

It is worth pointing out, and this is just one such fine example when the fifty-two corbels running the 41.1 meters (135 feet) frieze of the façade and the frontispiece had to be replaced. Apart from posing a major safety challenge to be changed, this involved an enormous expense as well.

It is when such dedicated volunteers come into the picture and make a huge difference. It all started when Toni Grima ordered 1,000 stainless steel clips from the UK. Enter then, Nenu Attard *tal-Impustat*, of JCR Ltd., who obtained the necessary pipes on loan from a very generous company Blockrete Ltd., for free.

A group of volunteers went directly to Malta and brought over 605 pipes, 300 clips and 300 connections from Blokrete Ltd., and loaded them on trucks provided by Raymond Attard, managing director of JCR Ltd.

These were transported and unloaded on the same day on the parvis of the Rotunda church. The scaffolding started on 7 July 2009 from 4 in the afternoon until 9 pm.

Kristinu Camilleri was then commissioned to do an exact copy of one of these corbels. The exceptionally talented

Kristinu took the precise measurements and did an exact pattern. In turn, he delivered a sculpted corbel within a hairline of the original.

Then Toni Grima and Ġużepp Pace worked out a fiberglass form to fit exactly the dimensions of the corbel, filled it with concrete and mixed it with the right color to match the stone itself. The result turned out excellent.

Fired with enthusiasm, the volunteers assembled the massive scaffolding rising to 25.9metres (85 feet) in height and running the 41.1 meters (135 feet) façade. They split into two groups of four men each: one with a concrete mixture, another with the wheelbarrow, and another with the vibrator so that the cement spreads evenly around. The fourth person used the electrical jigger to take out the old stone.

Altogether they used 130 kilos of stainless steel, 120 bags of white cement (JCR Ltd.), and six yards of sand and aggregate supplied by Vella Brothers *tal-Malla*.

Besides Toni Grima and Ġuzepp Pace, these proud volunteers were Felix Vella, Ġanni Spiteri, Charlie Attard, Leli Buttigieg, Charlon Buttigieg, Jonathon Azzopardi, Charles Borg and Luke Galea.

They were assisted by Toni Camilleri, Pawlu Attard, Jonathon and Anthony Attard from JCR Ltd., Anthony Buhagiar, Frans Debrincat and Vella Brothers.

A beautiful inscription in Roman letters was added to the façade: TEMPLUM SANCTO JOANNI BAPTISTAE DICATUM, which means, Temple dedicated to St. John the Baptist.

The late Kristinu's sons, Christopher and Johnnie Camilleri inscribed it. With this frieze, the façade became more striking and outstanding. (To further appreciate the work accomplished by these volunteers, please see the detailed plan of the timeline when the corbels were made and replaced on page 152.)

The *Vox Clamantis* choir needs excellent musical accompaniment. A very fine, sophisticated pipe organ, designed by Mr. Noel Gallo, has already been ordered and will be placed behind the main altar in the choir area.

The reason for the pipe organ to be placed here is threefold. Firstly, tests conducted on the site have found that the sound emanating from the presbytery is exceptionally superior. Secondly, the pipe organ is so big that it does not fit in the upper storey loft behind the main door that is reached via a double staircase.

Thirdly, the sound itself from the top storey loft would take too long before it reaches the choir. The pipe organ has been entrusted to Michael Farley Organ-Builders.

It will cost the princely sum of 276,000 euros and is due to be installed in the first quarter of 2016.

A small chapel on Soil Street, right at the bottom of Ċanga Street, is currently being built by J. Spiteri construction *tal-Pisklu*. This lovely chapel is envisaged to serve the spiritual needs of the numerous residents at ta' Ġokk area, a newly built section of Xewkija, nearest to Victoria.

Five levels of scaffolding for the refined pointing and sanding down of the strikingly beautiful Maltese stone

Chapter Nine

Shepherding the Flock

God never gives you more than you can handle.
Maria Assunta Mizzi

If I only have the will to be grateful, I am so.
Seneca

Entering the Rotunda today, the visitor is immediately struck by this truly monumental sacred place of graceful soft Baroque architecture. Its vastness is most impressive.

It is on a scale that is superbly proportioned and complements the sobriety of its classical ornament furnishings. The Rotunda is pure glory; it is one of the most interesting churches in Europe.

The eight equally distanced ferroconcrete Corinthian pillars, upon which rests the sheer perpendicular downward thrust of the 45,000 tons dome, is a supreme example of the high craftsmanship and absolute engineering genius.

These magnificent limestone covered columns surge up to 13.5 meters (45 feet) and are crowned with elaborate head cornices. These columns are probably the chief beauty that distinguish the Rotunda and further harmonizes the shape of the whole church. They represent the Eight Beatitudes of the Sermon on the Mount.

Its dynamism and volumetric connections result from the exuberant treatment of features. These include pediments, cornices, apses, lunettes and shells that add a delight in unexpected effects of angle and perspective and unite all so perfectly and seamlessly. These explicitly account for the excellent workmanship of this temple.

Likewise, the interior, although restrained, gives a great impression of elegance and lightness, thereby illuminating the splendid, refined limestone, invoking more space and distance.

This is mainly attributed to the sixteen clear glass, large windows of the dome and another attractive sixteen smaller ones in the lantern.

One can carefully observe the imposing dimensions and undulations of the curved and finely dressed *globigerina* limestone. These are all lined to perfection and formed into harmonious, geometric compositions of unparalleled splendor. It further makes the vast structure a celebration of the glories of God's creation.

To view the grandeur of the hemispherical dome, one has to crane his/her neck upwards to appreciate the impressive dome, rising a staggering 75 meters (246 feet) up to the lantern.

The marble flooring was all entrusted to the reputable firm A.F.Ellis
Courtesy Joseph Pace

At the same time, many wonder how a tiny, primitive village was able to build such a grand monument on a shoestring budget, in just two decades with 'a shilling and a dozen eggs'.

"*Beauty*," wrote the great contemporary philosopher and writer Roger Scruton, "*is the remedy of the chaos and suffering in human life...The beautiful work of art brings consolation in sorrow and affirmation in joy*".

The visitor can now appreciate three new rich, multicolored stained glass decoration windows. Two are on the lateral sides above the transept chapels and another in the triumphant arch of the façade; these give the Rotunda a warm dimension that transcends history.

Chevalier Paul Camilleri Cauchi designed these huge half-moon windows that were manufactured by '*Domus Dei P.D.D.M.*' of Rome. The artist Alessia Catallo collaborated on the project.

One depicts the Visitation of Mary to Elizabeth; the other is The Accomplishment of St. John the Baptist's mission as heralded by the Prophets.

The third one in the triumphant arch, high above the main door, is the Glorification or Apotheosis of St. John the Baptist, 2008 (2.77 by 5.59 meters or 9 x 18 feet). It depicts the Trinity and Christ himself welcoming the Baptist to the glory of heaven, flanked by the respective parents of John and Jesus.

According to Dr. Aaron Attard-Hili, these lunettes stained glass windows "*were meant to be his opus magnum in this genre ... where the glow of the spectrum of colors illuminated by shafts of sunlight pays homage to the skillful artistic thought underlying the whole scheme.*"

Indeed, these stained glass windows present a striking silhouette, particularly when the bright sunlight powers through them and the figures, robed in spectacular and colorful drapery, stand out in their full glory.

Six equally fine paintings are all the works of this celebrated Gozitan artist Chevalier Paul Camilleri Cauchi, (b.2.12.1940) figlio d'arte and most worthy son of Chevalier Wistin Camilleri (1885 – 1979).

Between father Wistin, and son Paul, they have the largest portion of all the high art and sculpted statutes exhibited in the Rotunda. It is truly a tour de force.

These geometric compositions are above the six side altars and measure 4.88 by 2.44 meters (16 x 8 feet). The linearity of these altar panels are well twinned and acquire meaning particularly along the graceful lines of this glorious temple.

The keen observer will note the chiaroscuro of the brush which exudes confidence and courage of Cartesian geometry onto the landscape. Their originality is also representative of this highly experienced artist in the sacred art.

The translucent effect heralds the triumph of Camilleri Cauchi. The way he achieves light and shade in portraying delicate silk and satin drapes and his handling of soft pastel shades to deeper tones of color is magnificent.

As mentioned earlier, the designs for the altar's grand perspectives were done by Ġuże' Galea, of Rabat, Malta.

The grisaille paintings of the four Evangelists (monochrome mixed media) above the two doors between the chapel of the Blessed Sacrament and the Sacristy are considered to be four of Camilleri Cauchi's best works.

A simple, clockwise tour (as marked in numbers on the back page). It starts from the narthex, [1] where there is a marble plaque with the history of the Rotunda: the blessing of the very first stone up to its solemn dedication. Next to it is the door leading to the winding staircase to the loft and roof level.

Two old stone statues [2] facing each other are from the façade of the old church, one of Zacharias, father of John the Baptist and the other of Elizabeth, his mother. These statues were both sculpted by Liberat Borg (1889). The Blessed Virgin Mary of Sorrows is in this chapel. This statue is from the prestigious firm of *Gallard et Fils* (1860).

In the chapel beyond the east door, [3] is the first of the six colorful paintings depicting the salient points of the life of John the Baptist, by Chevalier Paul Camilleri Cauchi. It begins with the Apparition of Archangel Gabriel to Zacharias in the Temple (1980). [4] Another fine statue from the firm *Gallard et Fils* (Marseille, France 1890) is the exquisite Blessed Virgin Mary of the Rosary. This figure has a broad religious significance in Xewkija and as a consequence a large number of faithful devotees.

[5] Nearby is the wooden sculpture of the Statue of St. Anthony, by the well-established firm from Tirol, *Insam N.Prinoth* (Tirivolo, Austria, 1906).

The second painting [6] in the immediate recess is the Birth of the Baptist in Hebron (1979). Upon close examination, this picture reveals that St. Anna's face is that of a most benevolent Xewkija donor, who lived to the venerable age of 94.

Below are the classic confessionals manufactured from pure selected mahogany by Mario Portelli from Qala. The statue of Christ beneath the Cross is by Alfred Camilleri-Cauchi (1985).

In the niche next to the confessional is the priceless statue of the prophet Elias, [7] sculpted in wood, by Marjanu Gerada (1790).

The writer remembers the late Emmanuel Fiorentino, who was then the chief art critic of The Sunday Times for many years, remarking that this statue represents the apex of master Gerada.

The following apse [8] is the Blessed Sacrament Chapel with a sumptuous Baroque tabernacle adorned with inlaid marble, dating back to 1678. It has a finely polished turnable shrine, also called *girandola*.

The majestic 17th-century marble altar was generously bequeathed to the parish of Xewkija, by Bishop Molina himself. It formerly belonged to the Mdina Cathedral Chapter. This precious refined multicolored marble altar (1755) is the primary altar of the old church.

The dominating painting above this chapel depicts St.John the Baptist in the Jordan Valley indicating the Lamb of God (*Ecce Agnus Dei* 1978).

The downward thrust of the 45,000 tons dome

The next door [9] is the entrance to the panoramic elevator and the very impressive Sculpture Museum. Above this door are two rectangular paintings (already mentioned) in mixed monochrome media. These are the Evangelists St. Matthew and St. Mark.

Next is the austere presbytery [10]. The beautiful white, limpid stone sculpture is by Kristinu Camilleri. Meanwhile the sculpted decoration of the marble high altar in *Bianco di Pietrasanta*, weighing several tons, is the work of Roman sculptor, Romeo Cecchotti (1974).

This richly decorated altar showcases the Lamb of God flanked by two beautiful angels beneath this pure white marble table, restrained at the corners by four bronze evangelists.

The ambone (or tribune) and the celebrant's chair are made of the same marble and designed by the same reputed firm, Romeo Cecchotti.

The Rotunda boasts some of the best Maltese limestone in the world

These were both carved and sculpted by the well-known Maltese marmista Ronald Pisani, in 1978. Pisani is an extraordinary master craftsman and has executed marble works of exceptional quality.

The choir [11] has ample seating for the *Vox Clamantis* choir and soon will host the magnificent pipe organ. High above is a triptych for the choir panels by Chevalier Paul Camilleri Cauchi.

These are the Holy Crucifix (1977) measuring 4.9 by 2.9 metres (16 x 9.5 feet), depicting The Dead Christ hanging on the Cross between another two rectangular paintings: Our Lady of Sorrows comforted by St. John the Evangelist (1988); and that of St. John the Baptist declaring Our Lord the 'Lamb of God' (1977).

The next door is the entrance to the sacristy [12]. Above this door are the next two Evangelists St. Luke and St. John the Evangelist, mixed monochrome media,

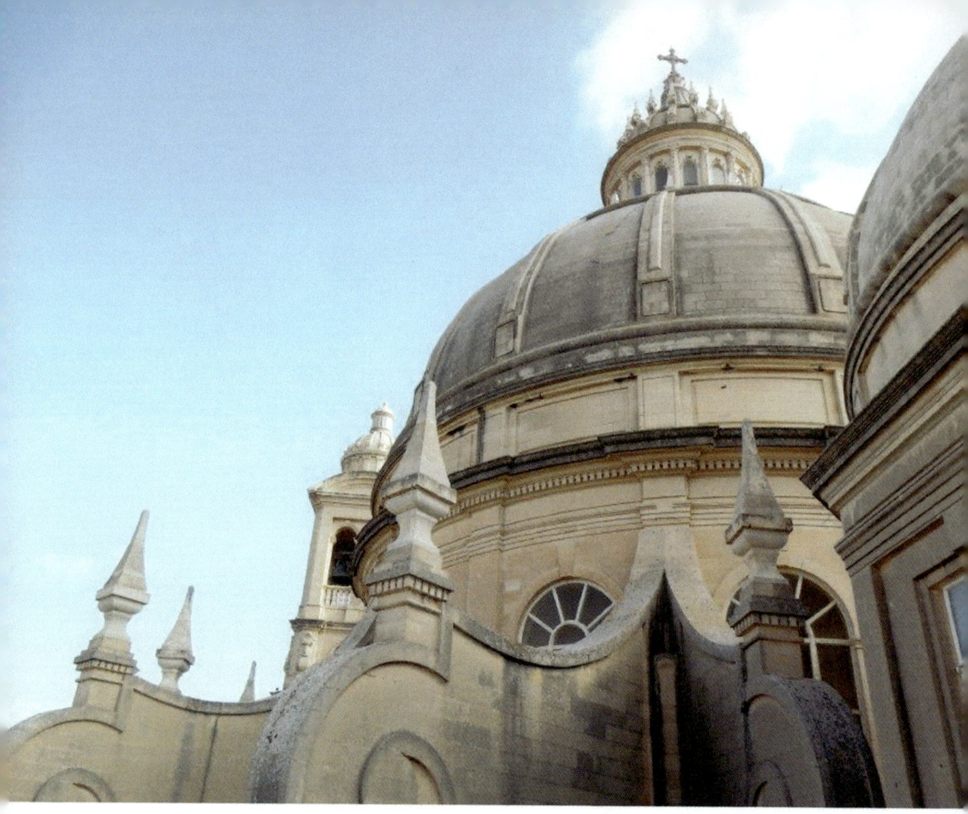

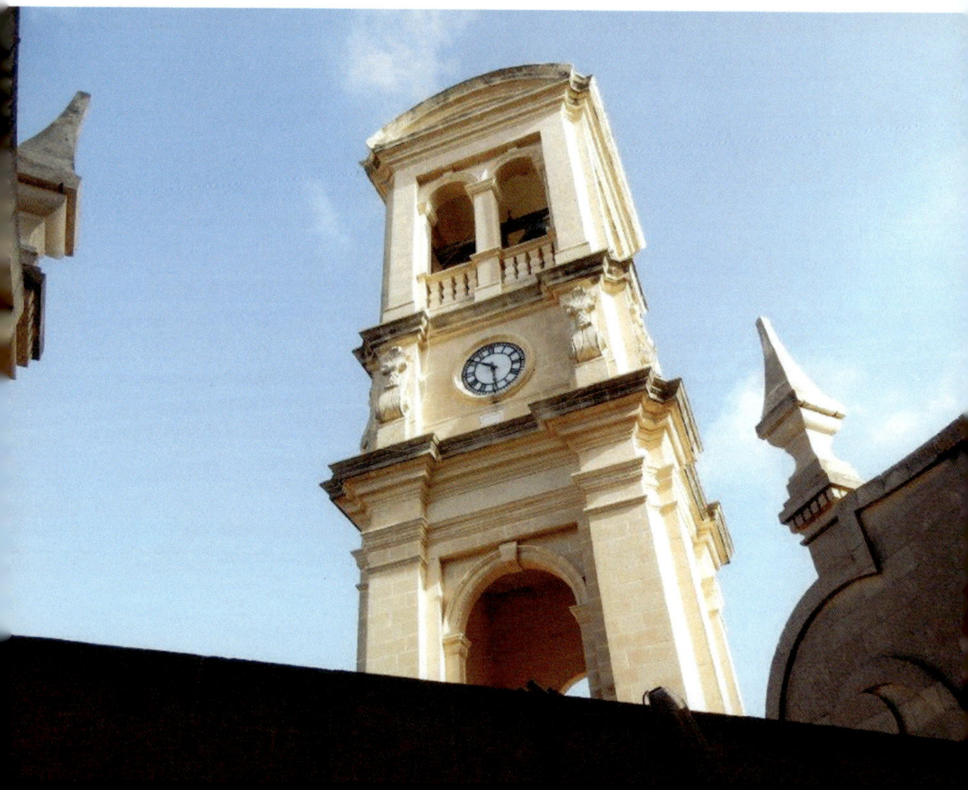

raised on a short plinth with gold leaves and low tones of tints streaming down in the background.

The vestry is decorated with the portraits of the fourteen Xewkija parish priests and archpriests from 1678 onwards, as referred to earlier. These also include the photos of the two young local patriots: Pawlu Vella and Salvu Azzopardi, who from this Temple entered into the bosom of our Heavenly Father.

At the back wall of the vestry is the statue of the Crucifixion by Chevalier Wistin Camilleri, (Għajn Qatet, Rabat, 1922).

The following apse [13] is the precious wooden Baptistery and the Baptismal font dating 1740 from the old church. High above, dominating the Baptistery is the remarkable painting of the Baptism of Christ by St.John the Baptist another work by Camilleri Cauchi.

The next niche [14] holds the statue of the Blessed Virgin Mary of Mount Carmel, sculpted in wood. Since this statue was massive to carry shoulder high during processions, a lighter one was acquired (Our Lady of Sorrows), and hence the name appellation was changed to that of Mount Carmel.

Above the second set of confessionals [15] is the painting of St. John the Baptist rebuking King Herod (1979). In the middle is a fine statue by Chevalier Wistin Camilleri depicting Christ in the Garden of Gethsemane (1922).

The next niche [16] holds the wooden sculpture of the Apostle St. Andrew. This statue is also from the firm *Insam N. Prinoth* (Trivolo, Austria, 1906).

The last painting by Camilleri Cauchi is probably his best work [17]. It is the powerful rendition of the martyrdom, the Beheading of the Baptist in Prison (1980).

Beneath is the life-size statue of St. Joseph by the French firm *Gallard et Fils* (Marseille, 1890). It is a delicate statue of an olive brown skin St. Joseph holding his Son. It is considered to be one of the oldest and finest on the island.

The west door [18] is immediately followed by the apse

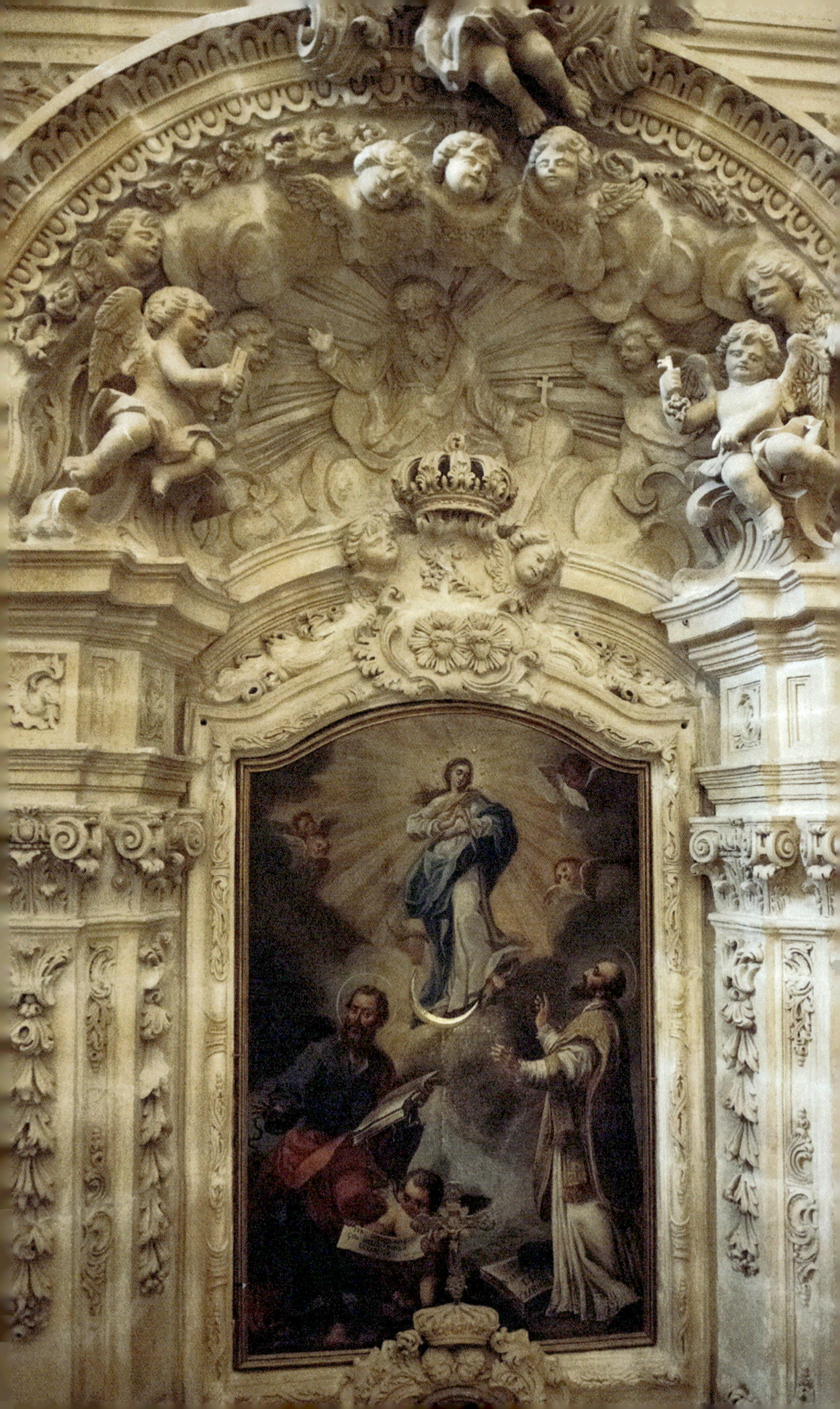

(19) holding the titular statue of St.John the Baptist. The *Prekursur* is standing high on a massive golden plinth, which expensive gilded plinth, was made by Paolo Bugeja (1899). As stated earlier, this truly beautiful statue of such an important religious figure was sculpted by the renowned Pietro Paolo Azzopardi (1845).

With his outstretched right hand, John, the itinerant preacher, points out Jesus and proudly proclaims Him as the Lamb of God (*Ecce Agnus Dei*). John motions this with his index forefinger. This precious statue is the great joy of all the *Xewkin*.

St. John the Baptist was a relative of Jesus. His mission was to preach repentance and prepare for the coming of Jesus Christ into public ministry. Following the baptism of the Lord, St. John the Baptist was imprisoned by Herod Antipas for speaking out against Herod's unlawful union with Herodias, the wife of Herod's brother, Philip.

On his birthday, Herod celebrated with a great feast. Salome, the daughter of Herodias, danced before the guests and charmed Herod. In gratitude, Herod swore to give Salome whatever she would ask, up to half his kingdom.

Salome, on the advice of her wicked mother Herodias, requested the head of John the Baptist on a platter. Herod regretfully ordered the execution. St. John the Baptist is the last and greatest of the Old Testament prophets.

The feast is celebrated on the third Sunday of June with immense veneration, pomp and well-organized celebrations and processions.

Inside, the church is bedecked in expensive sateen woven damask and sumptuous liturgical vestments. The main altar is covered with fresh, local and imported bouquets of flowers and plants.

Church bells break into frequent ten-minute joyful peals, loud peals that give one goosebump and make one's arm hair stand on end with excitement.

A special orchestra for this special occasion plays sacred polyphonic music while a baritone sings the famous *Ingresso Zaccaria*. The orchestra is backed up by the

A monumental apse adorned in fine Baroque Rococo over the Immaculate Conception

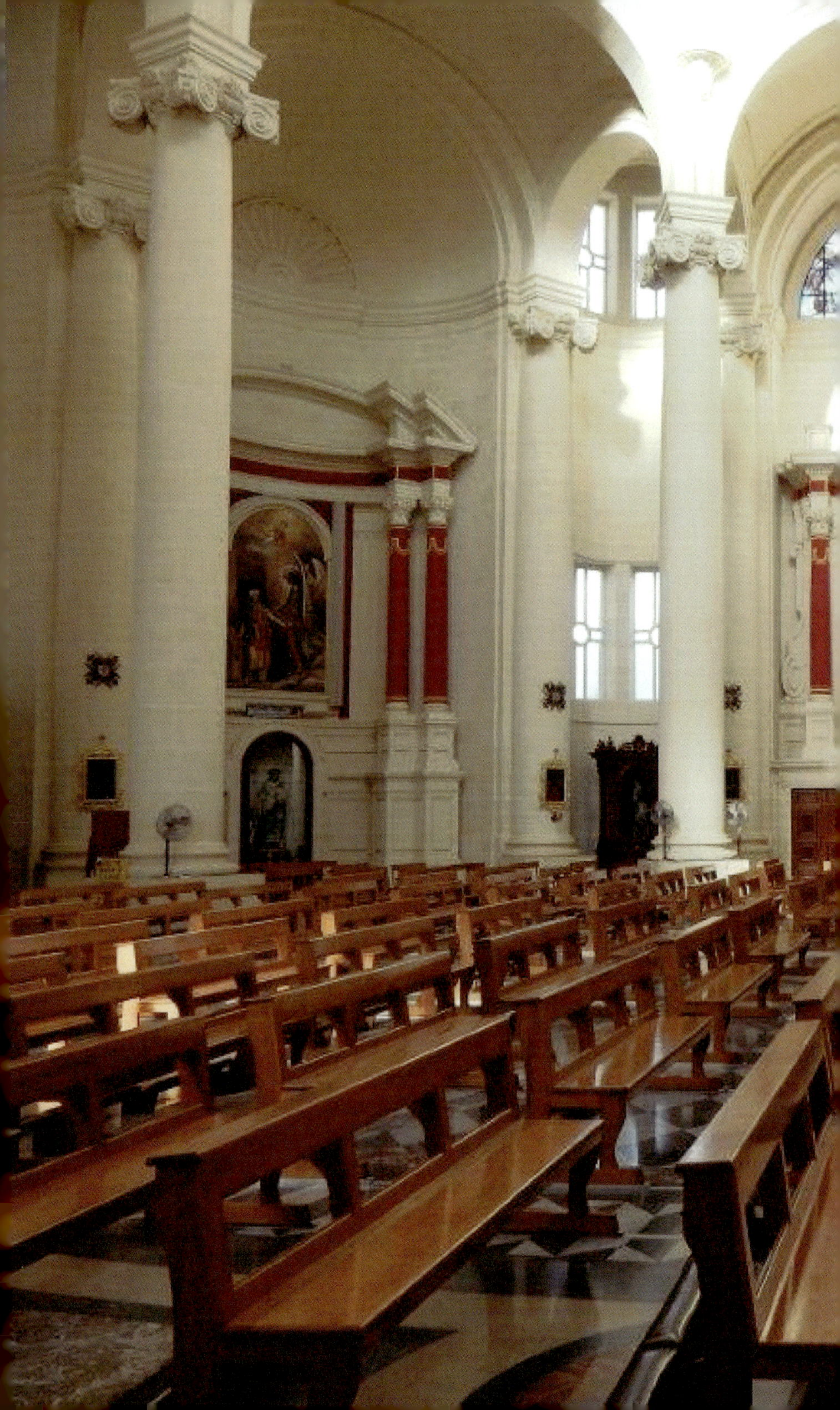

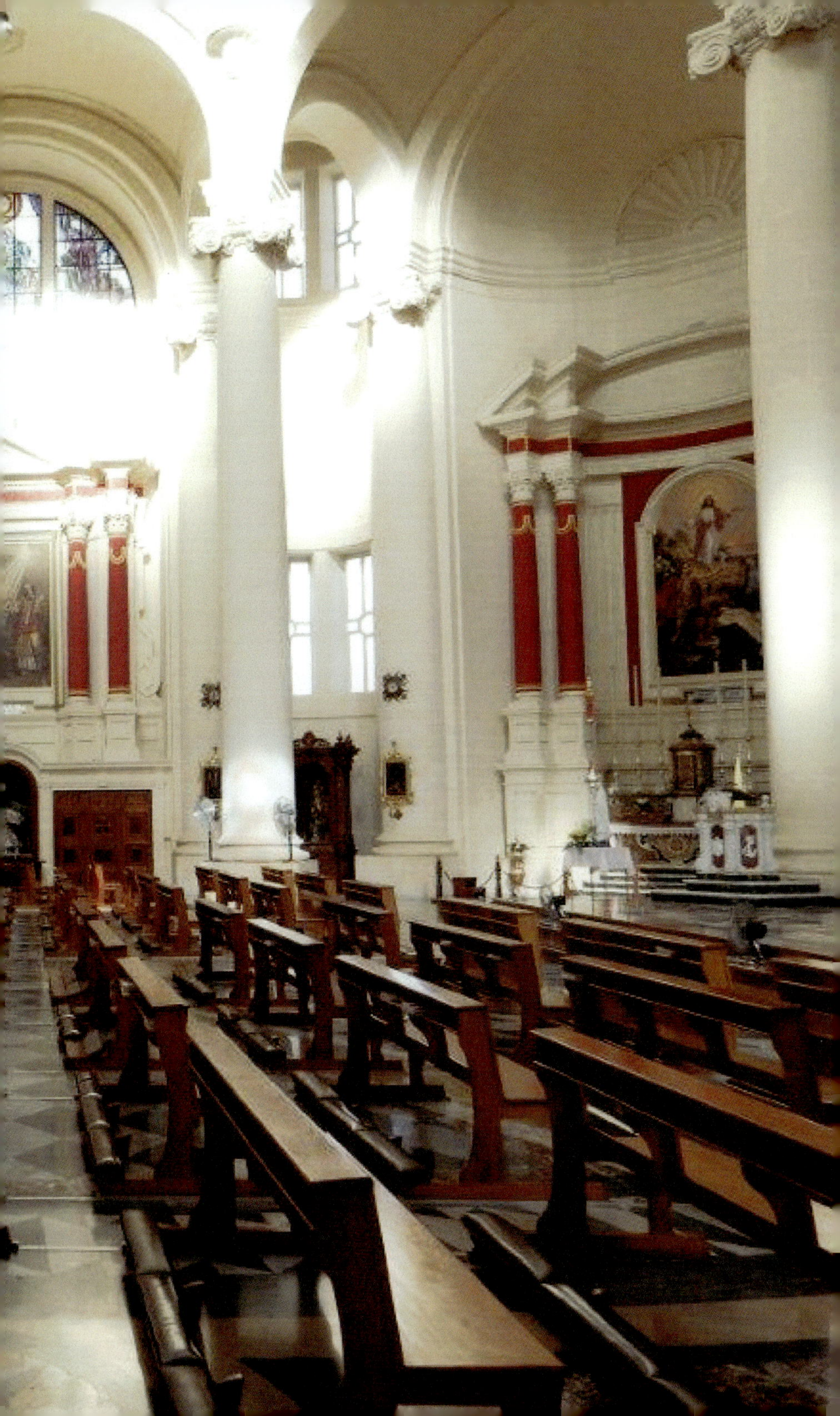

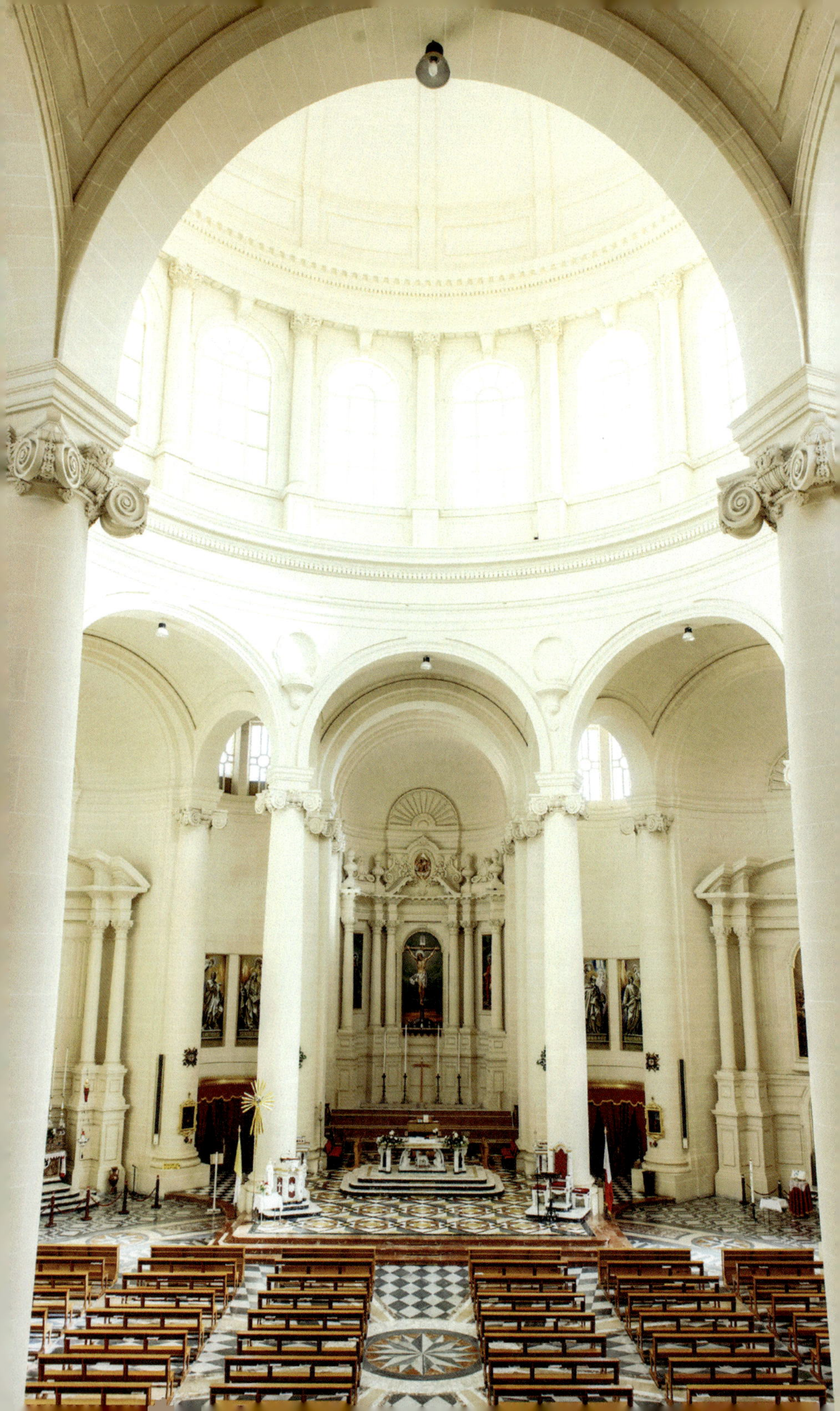

Pages 138-139 The austere interior of the Rotunda

splendid *Vox Clamantis* choir. (The *Te Deum* is sung on Saturday evening).

Then, the *Prekursur* band accompanies the magnificent statue taken shoulder high in a solemn procession around the village streets, accompanied by the recital of special prayers to the Baptist while the church is thronged with devout faithful.

Outside, amidst fireworks and petards and bands playing, children with nougat, scurry about in all their flamboyant finery.

Scores of teenagers in fluorescent T-shirts, who after gulping the ninth pint, try to staunch the impending hangover.

Meanwhile, their nattily dressed older couples chomp quietly on pastizzi with a beer can firmly in hand, under a mammoth, three- storey high umbrella, that covers a great part of the piazza circus.

Back inside the Rotunda, below, flanked by the magnificent statue of the Baptist, are two monuments. These are the life-size bronze busts, one of which is that of the much-beloved pioneer, Archpriest Ġużeppi Grech (1946-71) who conceived the idea and constructed the majestic Rotunda. A concise inscription reads:

*This temple bears
witness
to his resourcefulness.*

The other bust is of the immortal Ġuże' D'Amato (1951-1963), the church's eminent chief designer and architect. Underneath one finds an inscription written by none other than the prolific Gozitan poet, Ġorġ Pisani:

*Architect of great ability
drew out this harmony
from the heart of the Gozitan stone.*

The organ loft, [20] is just above the main entrance via the internal spiral stairway. The stone inscription [21] records the 300 years of the parish foundation (1678 - 1978). It also marks the Spiritual Seat of the Sovereign Military Order of the Knights of St. John's decision to

The main entrance to the Rotunda

make the Rotunda, their spiritual seat on the island of Gozo (22 March 1978). A warm red Maltese cross is on top of the façade. It is lit up during the night.

The Sculpture Museum is accessed through the east door [9] of the presbytery. It boasts several fine paintings. Chiefly these are the main altarpiece oeuvre by Gioacchino Loretta, and several wonderful pictures representing Our Lady of the Rosary, the Immaculate Conception, *Madonna del Buon Consiglio*, and Zacharias and Elizabeth (the father and mother of John). These are all by the reputed Francesco Zahra (1710 - 1773).

Zahra was Malta's most important native painter of the mid-18th century, and his decorative style is said to capture the spirit of the late Baroque.

On the left-hand side (clockwise) vestibule is the panoramic elevator [22]. The visitor will come upon three unusual honey-colored squared stones [23] with an enigmatic triangle jutting out carrying an engraved opulent fan inside.

Detail of one of the three altars found in the Museum of Sculpture

Their size is slightly bigger than a large pizza box but much thicker. Another similar set of two stones is lined across the hall inside the base of another altar.

These stones were once dug up during the foundations of the museum and most likely date back to the megalithic temple that once stood in prehistoric times, at *Magħqad ix-Xiħ*. The tessellated marble floor is a marvel to behold. These are the original old sepulchral slabs from the old church.

Next is the altar [24] of the Prophet Elias with a statue of St. Rita by Chevalier Wistin Camilleri (1924). This statute has replaced the one dedicated to the prophet that is now in the Rotunda as indicated earlier.

The prestigious painting of the Blessed Virgin Mary of the Rosary, [25] flanked by St. Dominic and St. Catherine of Siena, on their knees in adoration is by Francesco Zahra.

This rare painting is over the altar that was once in the western transept of the old church. According to Paul Falzon, it is one of the few paintings that Zahra signed (c. 1750).

144 - The Rotunda

Two showcases ([26] and [28]) across from each other, house a variety of cherished antiques and precious ecclesiastical memorabilia. Among these, are a bronze thurible (censer) in existence since the foundation of the parish, 27 November 1678, and a small silver sanctuary lamp dating back over 150 years.

One can also find the fine wooden bust of Jesus of Nazareth, carved by Marjanu Gerada, and an antique Book of Psalms. There is a rare set of six emerald green tumblers that were used during the feast of St. John, to illuminate the façade of the old church. These were lit using wax and candle oil; one had to climb high up a ladder to light these tumblers.

High above the main entrance of the Museum, [27] are two impressive paintings: the Birth and the Beheading of the Baptist, by Rokku Buhagiar (c. 1725 -1805). The latter is a faithful rendition of the famous painting by Caravaggio found at St. John's Co-Cathedral.

One of the two impressive paintings by Rokku Buhagiar (c.1725-1805) The Birth of the Baptist

These two masterpieces were checked for any deterioration in 2011 at the Studio Art Center International, in Florence, Italy. They were cleaned from dust and candle soot accumulated over the centuries. This timely restoration further enhanced their aesthetic qualities.

Rokku Buhagiar spent several years in Rome as a student in the Bottega of Giacomo Zoboli. He wanted to follow and emulate the style of Guido Reni. After returning to Malta in 1763, Rokku and his brother set up shop in Valletta.

The next painting [29] is above the altarpiece. It depicts the Holy Trinity with St. Gregory the Great and Our Lady interceding for the Souls in Purgatory. Its provenance is still unknown.

However, Alexander Bonnici O.F.M. Conv., points out that the painting bears a cartouche. It is the coat of arms of Grand Master Alof De Wignacourt (1547 - 1622), and that of Bishop Tumas Gargallo.

The Beheading of the Baptist by Rokku Buhagiar - a faithful rendition of the famous painting by Caravaggio

There is another coat of arms, of a donor (*ta' xi Donat*), of the Order of St. John, who hailed from Isla. For many years, this painting was in the east transept of the old church, at the altar of All Souls. It is highly treasured as it has high artistic and historical value.

The following altar, [30] is dedicated to the Immaculate Conception flanked by St. Paul and St. Ignatius of Loyola. Next to it is a niche with the Blessed Virgin Mary of Lourdes. The old choir, [31] now holds the main altarpiece of St.John the Baptist in the wilderness by Gioacchino Loretta (1637-1712), who hailed from the school of Mattia Preti.

This altar is flanked by two rectangular paintings featuring Zacharias and Elizabeth, the father and mother of St. John, both by Francesco Zahra.

The marble plaque (32), an eighteenth-century inscription
AUIERUNT – CREDIDERUNT – CUSTODIERUNT
It is found above the entrance door (9) and records the tradition of having heard the Apostle St., Paul, preaching from the island of Malta. St. Paul, together with the Evangelist St. Luke, planted the banner of Christianity on our islands. Surmounting this plaque is a splendid miniature painting of Jesus of Nazareth by Giuseppe Cali'.

Of great interest are fourteen Stations of the Cross imported in 1906. These are proudly hung around the church together with twelve marble crosses. These were enlarged by being inlaid with bronze Malta Crosses designed by Ġuże' Galea and made in the Stefano Sibellio factory in Carrara, Italy (1978).

It is befitting that in such a magnificent setting, worship should be offered with the greatest reverence and solemn respect.

Is it correct to say there is more beauty in an ancient Dolmen than a modern Trullo, more in El Greco or Van Gogh than in Frank Stella or Victor Pasmore?

"*Beauty can be consoling, disturbing, sacred, profane; it can be exhilarating, appealing, inspiring, chilling. It can affect us in an unlimited variety of ways. Yet it is never viewed with indifference.*" Roger Scruton concludes that "*Beauty is more than subjective; it is a universal need.*"

Meanwhile, if one happens to meet archpriest Mercieca, please consider yourself very fortunate indeed. Dun Karm, as he is affectionately known, together with the clergy, have spiritually shepherded the flock for the past 43 years.

During these four-plus decades, as a true spiritual guardian, archpriest Mercieca exemplified integrity, inspiration and, above all, kindness.

On 29th August 2015, on the Feast of the Martyrdom of St. John the Baptist, archpriest Mercieca together with the Mayor of Xewkija Paul Azzopardi, lit his last traditional bonfire in the main square.

The *Prekursur* Band ended playing their final anthem for the night while the Rotunda church glittered like an encrusted diamond on a fantastic August full moon rising.

The following day, on Sunday 30th, August Bishop Mario Grech announced that he had appointed Dun Karm as his Diocesan Director of Missions and Monsignor of the Cathedral Chapter. Half-heartedly, Dun Karm accepted his new call.

In the same breath, Bishop Grech announced that Monsignor Daniel Xerri from Xaghra is the new archpriest of Xewkija. Xerri was welcomed to great applause by all the parishioners present. Bishop Grech could not have made a better choice.

Mgr. Xerri was ordained a priest on 24th June 1994, precisely on the birth of the Baptist. He continued his studies in Rome where he obtained a doctorate in theology.

Daniel Xerri was appointed parish priest at Santa Maria della Pace parish in the Sabina-Poggio Mirteto diocese and later at Santa Maria Assunta parish in Corese Terra.

In 2004, Bishop Nicholas Cauchi called him back to Gozo and was duly appointed parish priest of San Lawrenz. Later, in 2007 Bishop Mario Grech appointed him as Rector of the Major Seminary of the Heart of Jesus, where he served until 2014.

Let us pray for our new Archpriest Monsignor Daniel Xerri to increase our faith and fill our minds with insight into love, so that every thought may grow in wisdom.

Lastly, the leitmotif of the heroic efforts of the past exemplifies the determination of a vast number of

Page 148-149
The Lamb of God flanked by adoring Angels; another capo lavoro found in the Museum of Sculpture

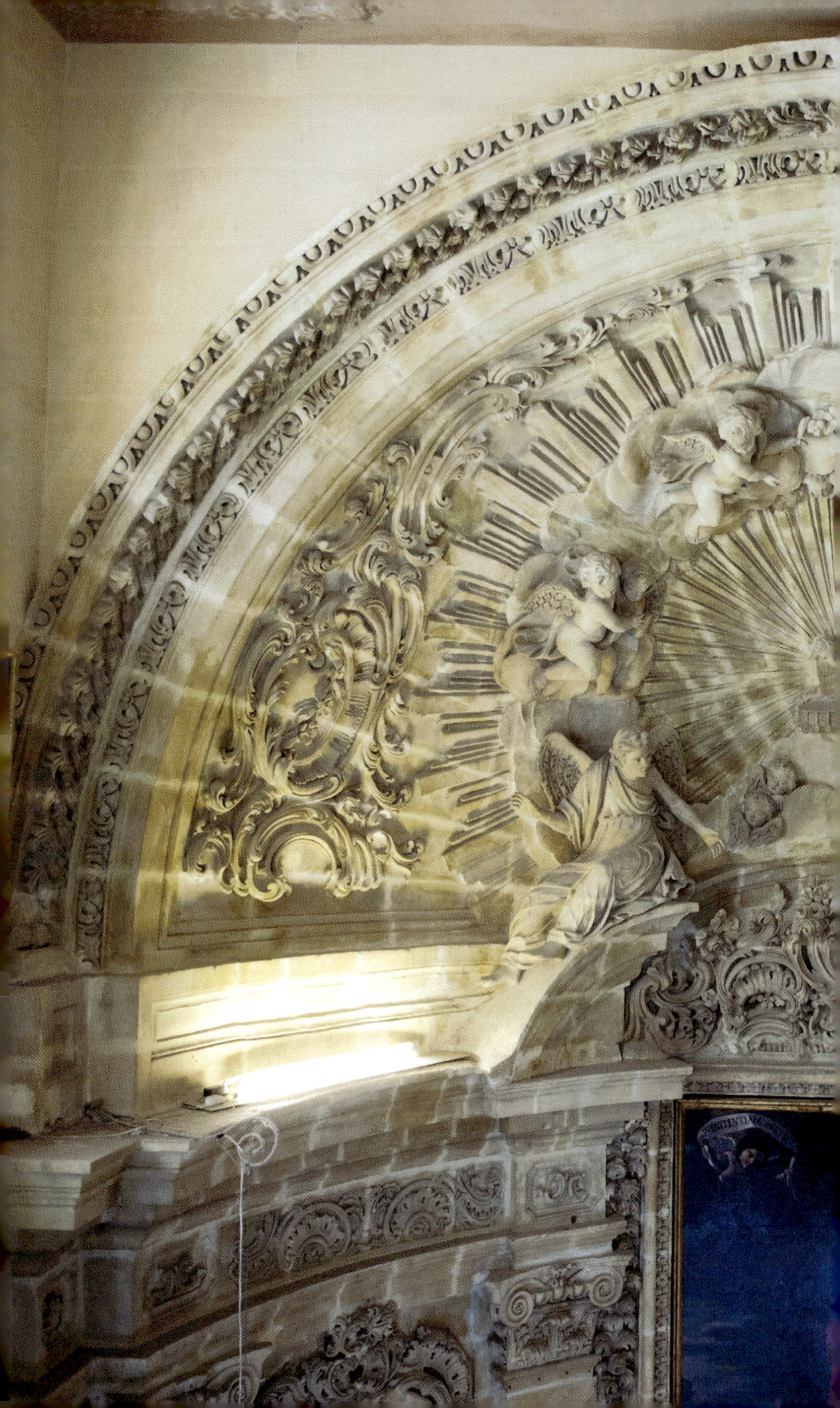

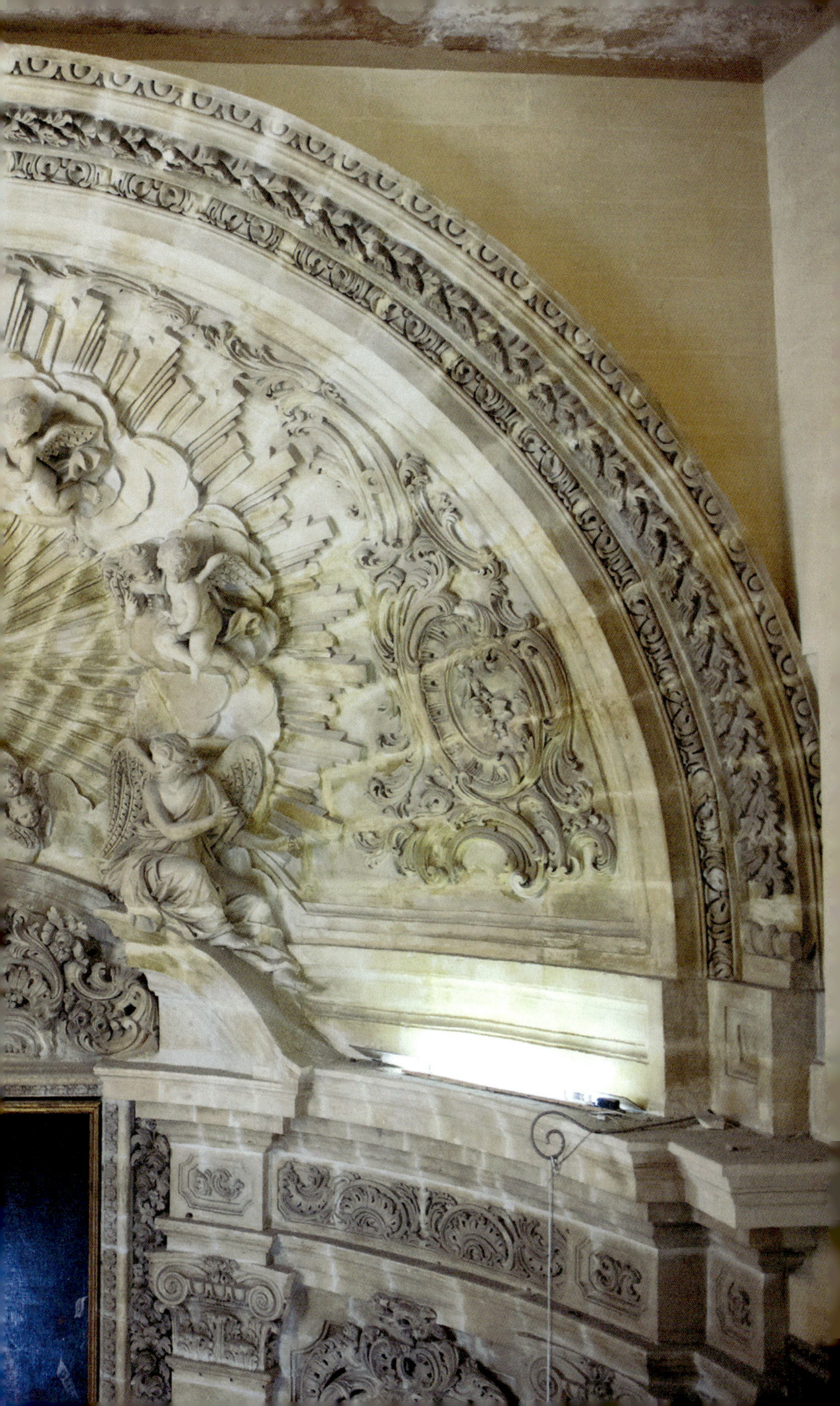

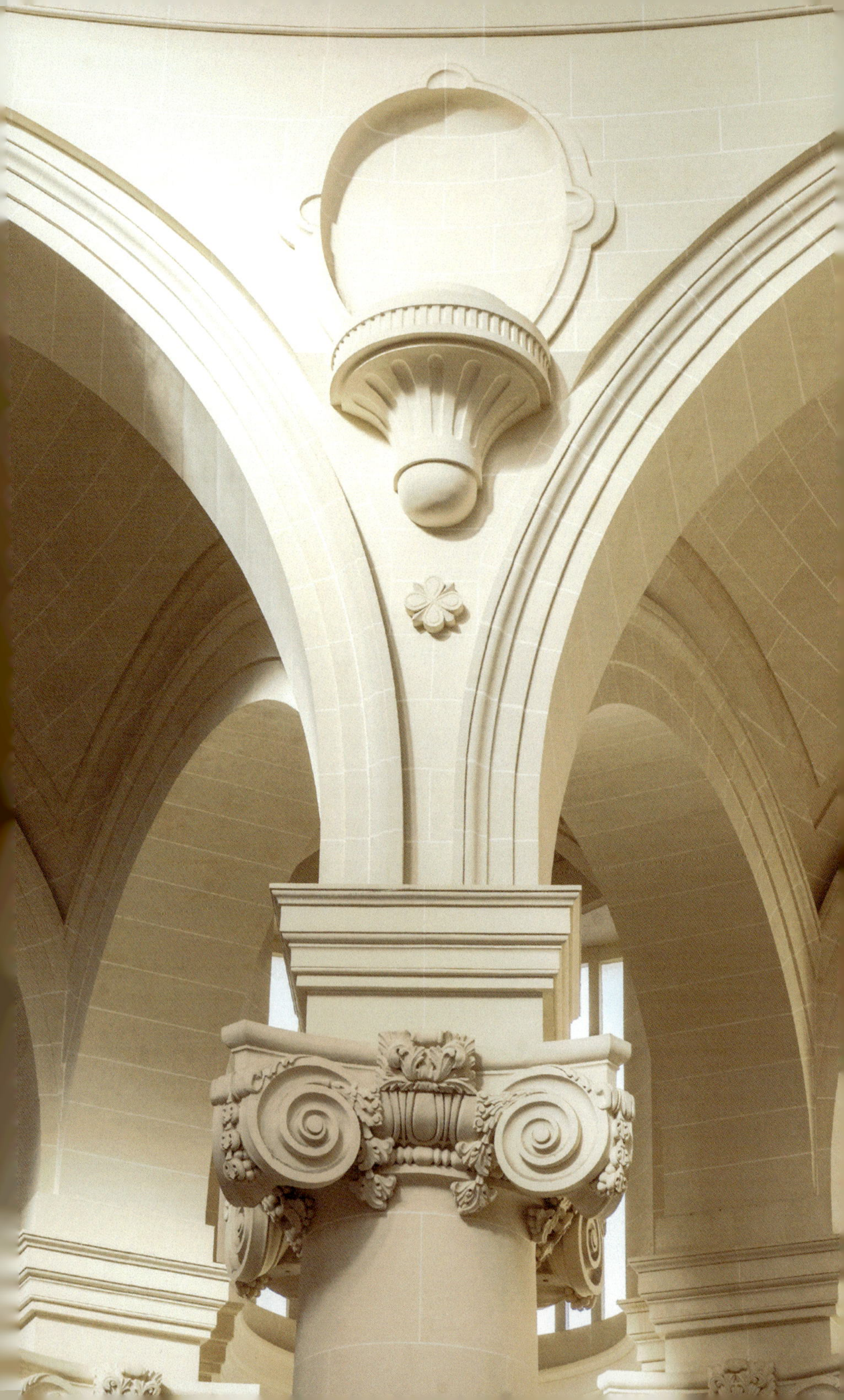

individuals. These benefactors help preserve the Rotunda as one of the great architectural and artistic national treasures of our islands. Many ponder about what the church meant then – and what it means today for our lives.

Our forefathers battled long and hard to see the Rotunda completed so as to move into a larger space where it is present. At each and every step, one can admire the grandeur, the power, and the goodness of God inside this church.

Although it is impossible to preserve everything, the most important things were painfully and carefully taken care. Thus, the historical importance of this landmark cannot be denied. The *Xewkin's* pride is entirely theirs, and it is well-earned, too.

However, that is not for the writer or anyone else to say. Let future generations decide.

Today, the beauty of the Rotunda church is there to raise our hearts and minds to heaven.

And like the sublime truth in the Gospel according to St. Mark, (4:21-25), the Rotunda is "meant to be put on a stand".

Let it shine like a lamp throughout the world to proclaim far and wide that God is One.

Four arches resting on one of the eight columns

Timeline of works
done by volunteers

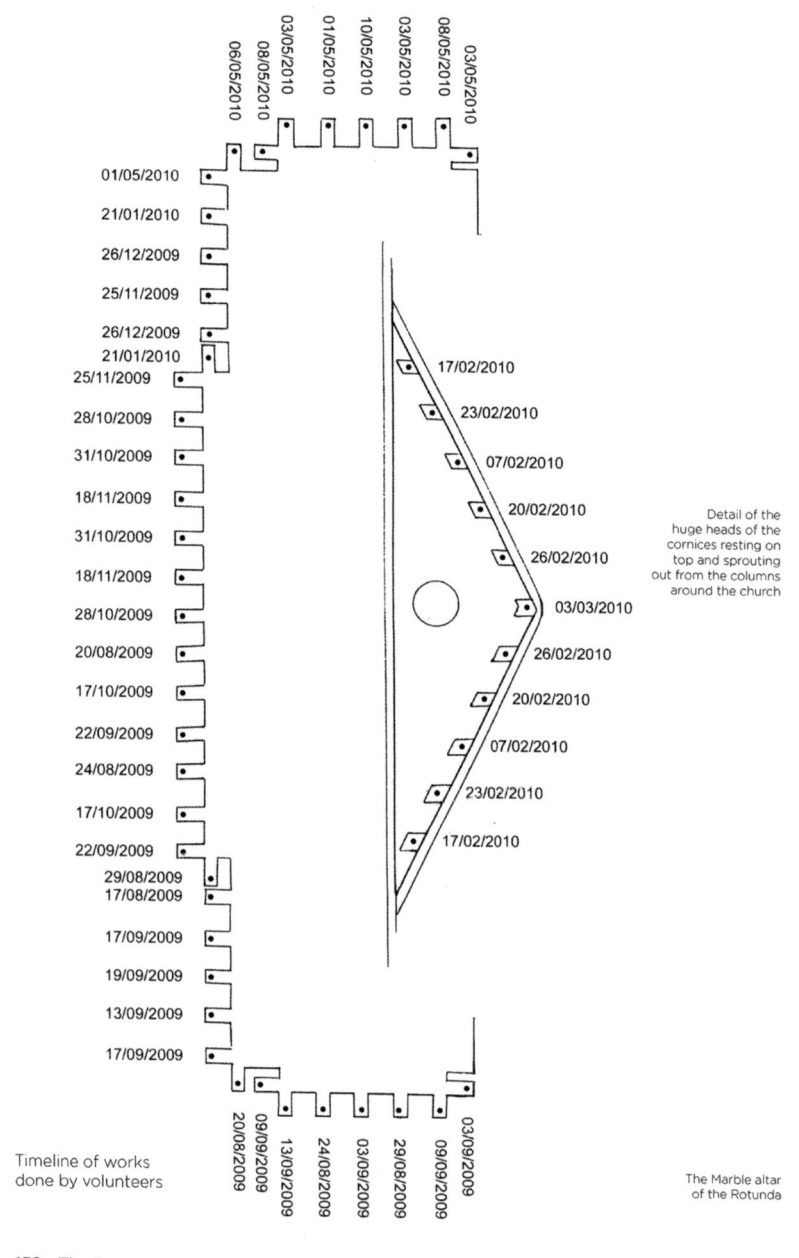

Detail of the huge heads of the cornices resting on top and sprouting out from the columns around the church

The Marble altar of the Rotunda

152 - The Rotunda

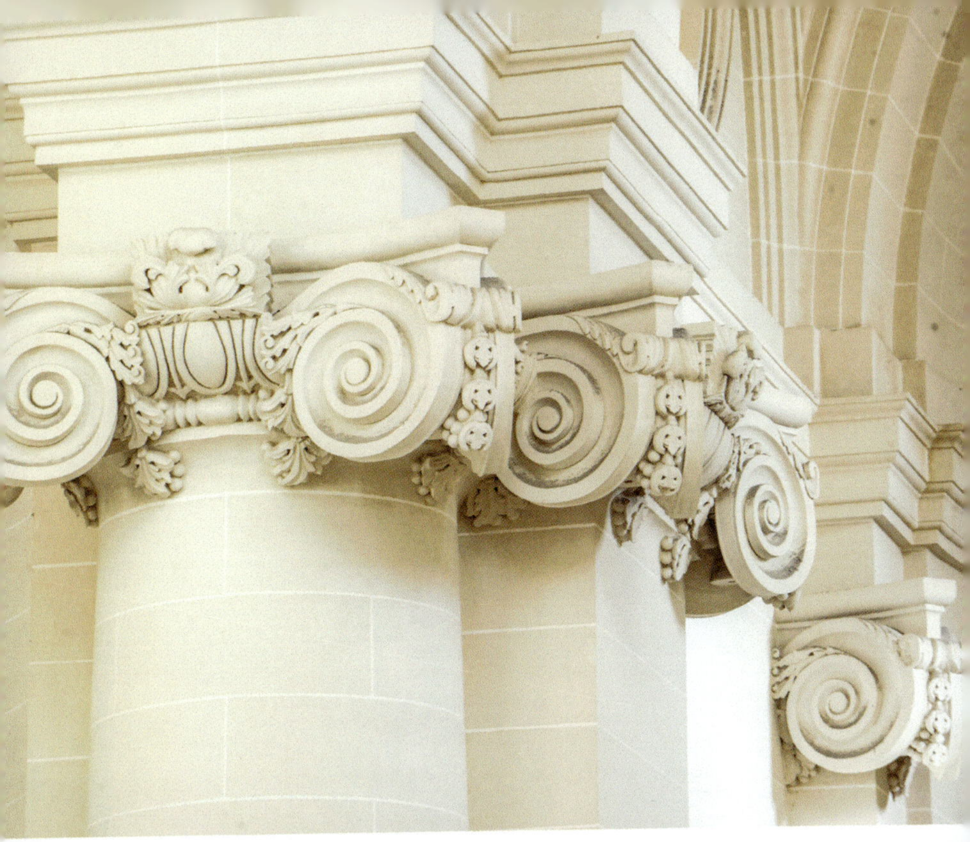

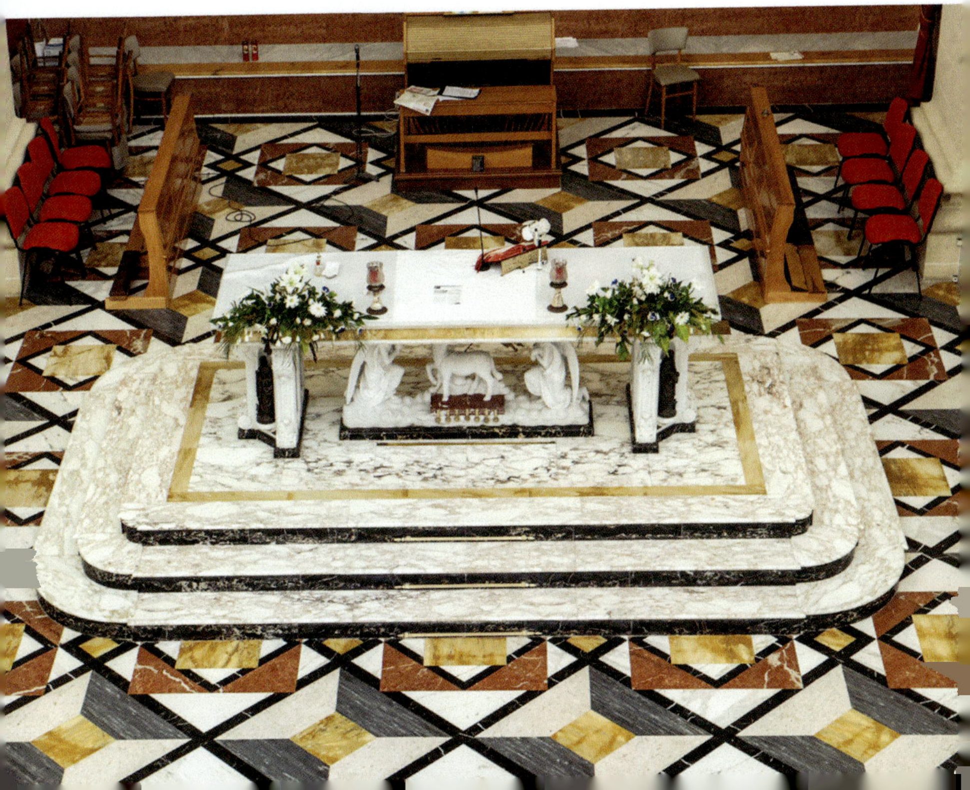

End Note

Back in 1973, little did I think that one day I will get to write this guide book. And that the main source of my research and valuable information would come out of an annual publication called Gourġion.

This magazine initially started out as a newsletter 42 years ago by none other than Dun Eddie Zammit ta' Beruka, today Rector of The Good Shepard Chapel, in Rabat. Dun Eddie was then head of the Presidium of the Legion of Mary consisting of five secondary school students including myself.

For a brief period, I gave a helping hand as assistant editor. The other students in the group were Carmel Attard tad-Dubra, Joe Xuereb tal-Bilbel (who passed away in the flower of his youth at 16 years of age), his cousin Dr. John Xuereb Curmi M.D. tal-Bilbel, and Arthur Bajada ta' Pressu.

Eddie was the Editor. Our meetings were held in a house at the beginning of San Bert Street. The typing was done on wax paper, and the printing itself was done by hand using a basic Gestetner stencil duplicator.

I submitted a couple of poems, one under the nom de plume, 'Anderson'. Meanwhile, I had already paid the fees to sit for my upcoming GCE exams. However, before I could take my exams, the force of destiny changed all that.

In early May 1974, I got an unexpected call from the Emigration Office in Rabat, to let me know that a seat was available on an Alitalia flight. Would I take it? I did not think twice.

In a matter of days and after paying five Maltese lira (the Government then subsidized the fare), I was crossing the Atlantic Ocean, heading out to New York.

NYC was the biggest city in the world. It was also on the brink of bankruptcy, laying off hundreds of sanitation workers, firefighters, police officers and all sorts of federal employees. I was 17.

Looking back, I guess that it is true that life is a long lesson in humility and that it eventually comes full circle. At least that is how it seems to be in my case. So it is with heartfelt thanks and greatest pleasure that I am now able to contribute a little bit more to the village of my birth before I turn the last few corners.

I arrived at JFK airport penniless since I had foolishly spent all my money on gifts while waiting at Malpensa Airport, Milan, for the connection flight en route to New York. And when I landed, there was no one waiting for me at JFK because my sister had not received the letter. (The post, in fact, arrived a day after my arrival).

However, that is another story. Those interested in obtaining a copy of the forthcoming book about the two decades plus in the Big Apple entitled, Along the Road with a Gozitano can do so by contacting the writer on tedmizzi@gmail.com

On a final and happy note, huge congratulations must go to our energetic Xewkija Tigers President, Jeffrey Farrugia tac-Cikkarell who together with a great team, a disciplined coaching staff and a dedicated committee regaled the numerous XT supporters by clinching three exciting Championships in the last four years. And this besides a host of other prestigious cups.

So Go On Be A 12th Tiger.

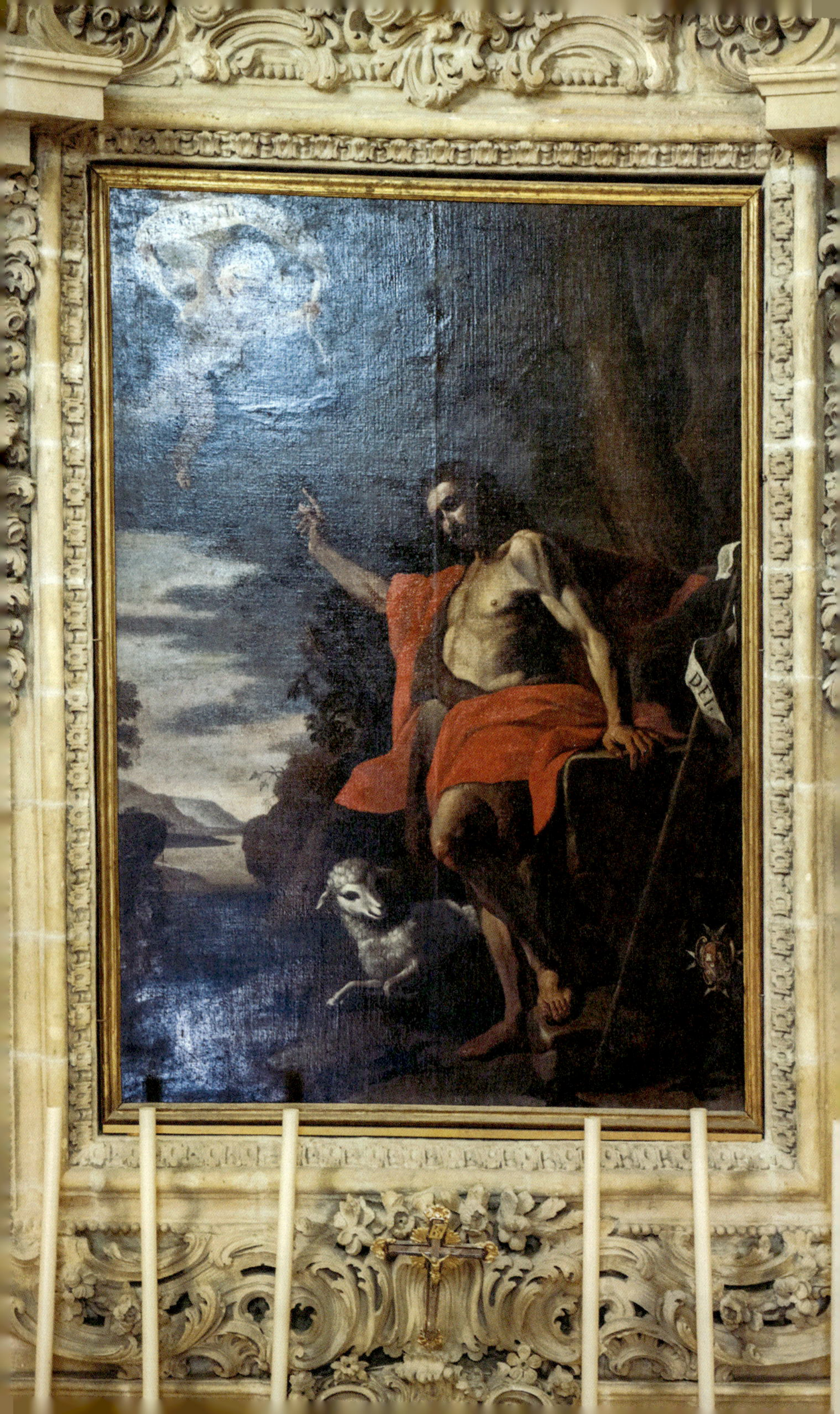
DEI

Art and Architectural terms used in the Guide

Apse: semi-circular vaulted space terminating the east end of a church
Archivolt: molding around an arch
Architraves: (main beam) in classical entablature, it is the lowest part of the entablature consisting of architrave, frieze, and cornice
Baldaquin: altar canopy supported on columns or hung from above
Baroque: the revolution in the arts that took place in Italy at the end of the 16c derives its name from the Portuguese word "barrocco" meaning something irregularly shaped (originally used of pearls). It affected all aspects of art – architecture, painting, sculpture – and also literature and music, giving rise to some outstanding masterpieces.
Barrel vault: simple, half-cylindrical vault
Capital: molded or carved top of a column supporting the entablature
Cartouche: ornamental panel with inscription or coat of arms (Baroque)
Chiaroscuro: treatment of areas of light and dark in a work of art
Cornice :(Italian meaning ledge) is any horizontal decorative molding that crowns a building along the top of an interior wall
Entablature: projecting upper part of building supporting the roof
Frieze: is the wide central section of an entablature and may be plain in the Ionic or Doric order, or decorated with bas-reliefs.
Globiġerina: quarried limestone blocks from sedimentary rock used as a building material and suitable for sculptural purposes because of its softness
Grisaille: monochrome painting in shades of gray
Lantern: windowed turret on top of a dome
Lunette: (French little moon) is a half-moon shaped place, either filled with recessed masonry or void. A lunette is formed when a horizontal cornice transacts a round-headed arch at the level of imposts, where the arch springs. The term is usefully employed to describe the section of an interior wall between the curves of a vault and its springing line. A system of intersecting vaults produces lunettes on the wall surfaces above a cornice. A lunette is commonly called a half-moon window when space is used as a window.
Narthex: rectangular vestibule between the porch and nave of a church
Ossuary: place where the bones of the dead are stored
Pendentive: triangular section of vaulting rising from the angle of two walls to support a dome
Perit: a graduate technical expert in building
Rib: projecting band separating the cells of a vault
Rococo: style in architecture, especially in interiors and the decorative arts, which originated in France and spread throughout 18th century Europe. In contrast with heavy Baroque grandiloquence, Rococo was an art of exquisite refinement and linearity.
Transept: wing or arm of a church at right angles to the nave
Triptych: a set of three panels or pictures, often folding and used as an altarpiece
Volute: spiral scroll on an Ionic capital

Rabat is the capital of Gozo unless otherwise mentioned as Rabat, Malta.

Dun is Rev., Fr. (used for diocesan Catholic priests, and followed by the Christian name).

The chiaroscuro of St John in the Wilderness by Gioacchino Loretta (c.1637 -1712) a gift of Bishop Molina

Photographer Max Xuereb during his photo session high up inside the dome.

New archpriest Mgr Daniel Xerri

158 - The Rotunda

TEMPLUM SANCTO JOANNI BAPTISTAE DICATUM

Essential Bibliography and Sources

Ix-Xewkija Tul Iż-Żmenijiet,
    Borg Fr. Serafin O.S.A., Mercieca Bennie, Vella Joseph J.,
    Calleja Nazzarenu, Zammit Haber Francis, Xuereb Joseph
    Orphans' Press, Għajnsielem, Għawdex.

Ix-Xewkija Fi Ġrajjiet Il-Kappillani u L-Arċiprieti Tagħha,
    Serafin Borg O.S.A., Progress Press Malta 1978

Ix-Xewkija 300 Sena Parroċċa 1678 – 1978,
    J.J. Vella, Editur

The Rotunda Monumental Church – Xewkija – Gozo
    by Joseph Xuereb, President of Xewkija Parish Council –
    A&M Printing Ltd., Qala 1984

See APX, Storia della Fabbrica delle Navate della Chiesa
    Arcipretali di Xeuchia, pp. 1-4

Gozo – A historical and tourist guide to the island,
    Mgr.Dr. Anthony Gauci - 1966

Xewkija – The First Village of Gozo,
    Joseph Bezzina – Gaulitana 23 – 2004

New light on Majmuna's tombstone,
    by Giovanni Bonello, LL.D. The Sunday Times, November 8, 1992

The Village of Xewkija and the Feast of St John the Baptist,
    Joe Zammit Ciantar - The Malta Independent on Sunday –
    23 June 2013

The Gourgion Tower,
    Joseph Calleja & Frans Zammit Haber – Gutenberg Press 1997

Landmark church in Gozo provides panoramic view facility for
    visitors, Michael Testa – The Times, Monday June 3, 2002

Malta Illustrata, Giovanni Francesco Abela – 1647

Ruins of a Megalithic Temple at Xeuchia (Shewkiyah) Gozo,
    First Report by Emmanuel Magri SJ –
    Edited by Charles Cini SDB – Heritage Malta

Malta, Gozo & Comino –
    Cadogan Island Guides, Simon Gaul – Cadogan Books Ltd. – 1993

The Academic Colorista,
    Paul Camilleri Cauchi, Editor Fr. Charles Cini SDB –
    Baroni & Gori, Prato, Italy 2014

Basilica della Salute, Venezia 2010 Edizioni KINA Italia/L.E.G.O.

Fortress – Architecture & Military History in Malta,
    Prof. Quentin Hughes – Date 2001 (re-print)

V. by Thomas Pynchon – Lippincott edition 1963

Management: Tasks, Responsibilities, Practices,
    Peter F. Drucker - Harper & Row, Publishers 1973

Chronicles – Volume One, Bob Dylan – published
    by Simon & Schuster 2004

Useful Quotations – A Cyclopedia of Quotations
    by Tryon Edwards, D.D. – Grosset & Dunlap, Publishers, New York

Maltese-English Dictionary
    by Joseph Aquilina published by Midsea Books Ltd. 1987

Oxford American Dictionary, Oxford University Press 1980

The Concise Columbia Encyclopedia, Columbia University Press 1981

The Vatican II Weekday Missal
    by the Daughters of St. Paul 1975 – Boston, Mass.

Ta' Pinu Shrine – The Pilgrims' Haven
    by Mgr. Nicholas J. Cauchi – 2008 - Gozo Press, Ghajnsielem

Wikipedia – the free encyclopedia

Artists of the Buhagiar & Zahra families,
    Dominic Cutajar The Times – October 3, 1980 PP4-5

Mario Attard - Rokku Buhagiar (1725-1805)
    Il-Pittur Li Jinsab Midfun Fil-Kunvent Ta' Santa Tereża Bormla

Treasures in Maltese Churches – Teżori fil-Knejjes Maltin –
    Victoria – Il-Fontana - Gozo by Tony Terribile

Ten places to see before they're changed forever
    by Tamara Hinson for CNN – March 25, 2015

The Great Temple 360 by Cynthia de Giorgio –
    Miranda Collection

Review of the History and Restoration of Xewkija Church Clock –
    Josmar Azzopardi – Soc.Filarmonika Prekursur Ħarġa No.9

Gourġion in annual chronological order:

1977 – Ħarsa lejn is-sena 1716 – Il-Parroċċa Tax-Xewkija Mill-Vista Pastorali Ta' L-Isqof Ġakbu Cannaves minn Alexander Bonnici O.F.M. Conv pp 2- 5

1978 – Il-Kwadru Titulari tax-Xewkija – xandira fuq Cable Radio 22-6-1975 minn Joe Camilleri pp 2 - 8

1979 – Il-Qagħda Tal-Knisja Parrokkjali Tax-Xewkija Fi Ftuħ Tas-Seklu XVIII minn Alexander Bonnici O.F.M. Conv. pp 9 - 11

1982 – It-torri Gourġion fix-Xewkija minn Alexander Bonnici O.F.M. Conv., H.E.D., S.T.L.., Ph.B. pp 11 – 13

1984 – Ix-Xewkija – Żviluppi Soċjali fuq Art iebsa biex tinħadem minn Alexander Bonnici O.F.M. Con., H.E.D., S.T.L. Ph.E. pp 4 -5

1986 – Ir-Rotunda Tax-Xewkija – xi dettalji li tajjeb tkun taf minn Wenzu Camilleri p 9

1993 –Toni Camilleri – L-iskultur Tax-Xewkija minn L.Camilleri pp 8-9

1995 – Ix-Xewkija l-Ewwel Raħal F'Għawdex minn Rev. J. Bezzina pp14-15; Is-sett ta' Pitturi tal-Knisja Parrokkjali tax-Xewkija – intervista ta' Ivan Farrugia p23

1997 – X'Niftakar Mill-Bini Tal-Knisja – Intervista ma' Żakkarija Cilia p 29

1998 - Pittura tal-Kav. Paul Camilleri Cauchi p 51

1999 – Il-Mużew tal-Iskultura jikteb Ġużeppi Xuereb pp 29-31; mir-reġistri tal-Parroċċa -p 51

2000 – Kwadri Antiki fil-Mużew ta' l-Iskultura – p 72

2002 – Il-Bidu tal-Bini tar-Rotunda – Sur Ġużeppi Xuereb u Dun Edward Xuereb pp 9-22; Intervista lil Ġużepp Vella – Bennej tal-Knisja Rotunda mill-Arcipriet Mons. Carmelo Mercieca pp23- 27

2003 – Deskrizzjoni Tal-Knisja l- Qadima Tax-Xewkija minn Dun Ġwann Grech pp15-19

2004 - Nhar il-Gimgħa 19 ta' Diċembru beda t-tqiegħed ta' l-ewwel filata ta' l-iskutella tal-Koppla ta' quddiem p 37; Mill-Arkivju tal-Parroċċa p 63

2005 - Dati ta' Tifkiriet pp 36-37; Opri Ġodda - Apprezzamenti p 67

2006 -Il-Knisja Parrokkjali tax-Xewkija li nbniet fis-seklu sbatax - Paul Falzon B.A. (Honours) History of Art pp 5-9; Xebħ fix-xogħol ta' Skultura kitba ta' Mario Fenech pp 27 - 29; Il-Proġett tal-Bini tal-Kopletta p 39; Il-Qniepen tal-Knisja Arċipretali ta' San Ġwann fix-Xewkija kitba ta' Kenneth Cauchi B.Cons (Hons) Kampanologista pp43 -48; Marija Grech Rebbieħa - 'Gieħ ix-Xewkija' p 90; Patri Serafin Borg O.S.A 50 Sena ta' Saċerdozju (1956 -2006) p 93

2007 - L-Inkwatru Titulari ta' San Ġwann Battista tal-Knisja l-Qadima tax-Xewkija - Kjarifikazzjoni tal-fatti - kitba ta' Paul Falzon B.A. (Honours) History of Art pp 41- 44; 9 ta' Ġunju 2007 Tberik tas-Salib u tal-Koppla ta' quddiem pp 48 - 49; Tagħrif dwar is-Salib tal-Koppla ta' Quddiem; Tagħrif dwar il-Koppla ta' Quddiem p 53; Apprezzamenti p 69; Il-qniepen issa f'posthom p 49

2008 - Francesco Vinċenza Zahra u l-pittura tiegħu fil-knisja l-Qadima tax-Xewkija - Kjarifikazzjoni tal-fatti - kitba ta' Paul Falzon B.A. (Honours) History of Art pp 9 - 12; Il-Glorja ta' San Ġwann Battista p 43; Marru jieħdu l-premju ta' ħidmithom p 61

2009 - Oġġetti esebiti fil-Mużew tal-Arkeologija ta' Għawdex misjuba fil-limiti tax-Xewkija - Stephen Cini pp 21 - 25; Kristu u Ġwanni mħabbra mill-Profeti u Iż-Żjara ta' Marija lil Eliżabetta pp 44-45

2010 - Ir-Restawr tas-Saljaturi tal-Faċċata tal-Knisja Rotunda minn Lulju 2009 sa Mejju - Mons. Carmelo Mercieca 2010 pp 23 - 27

2011 - Intervista lil Dun Ġwann Xuereb minn Bennie Mercieca pp 18 -21; Erba' Pitturi tal-Evanġelisti xogħol tal-Kavallier Pawlu Camilleri Cauchi pp 46 -47; Żakkarija Cilia - Kav. Żarenu Calleja u M'Angelo Camilleri p 61; Telqu Qabilna pp 73 - 75

2012 - 60 Sena mit-Tberik tal-Ewwel Ġebla tar-Rotunda pp 9 -11; L-Arloġġ tal-Knisja l-Qadima jerġa jibda jaħdem b'differenza, fil-Kampnar Maestuż tal-Knisja Rotunda tax-Xewkija - intervista ta' Bennie Mercieca lil Pullu Xerri pp 17 -19; lx-Xewkija: frak ta' storja u tifkiret oħra -- kitba ta' Dun Geoffrey G. Attard pp 21 - 23

2013 - Ġuże' D'Amato (1886-1963) Il-Perit tar-Rotunda tax-Xewkija pp 29 -30

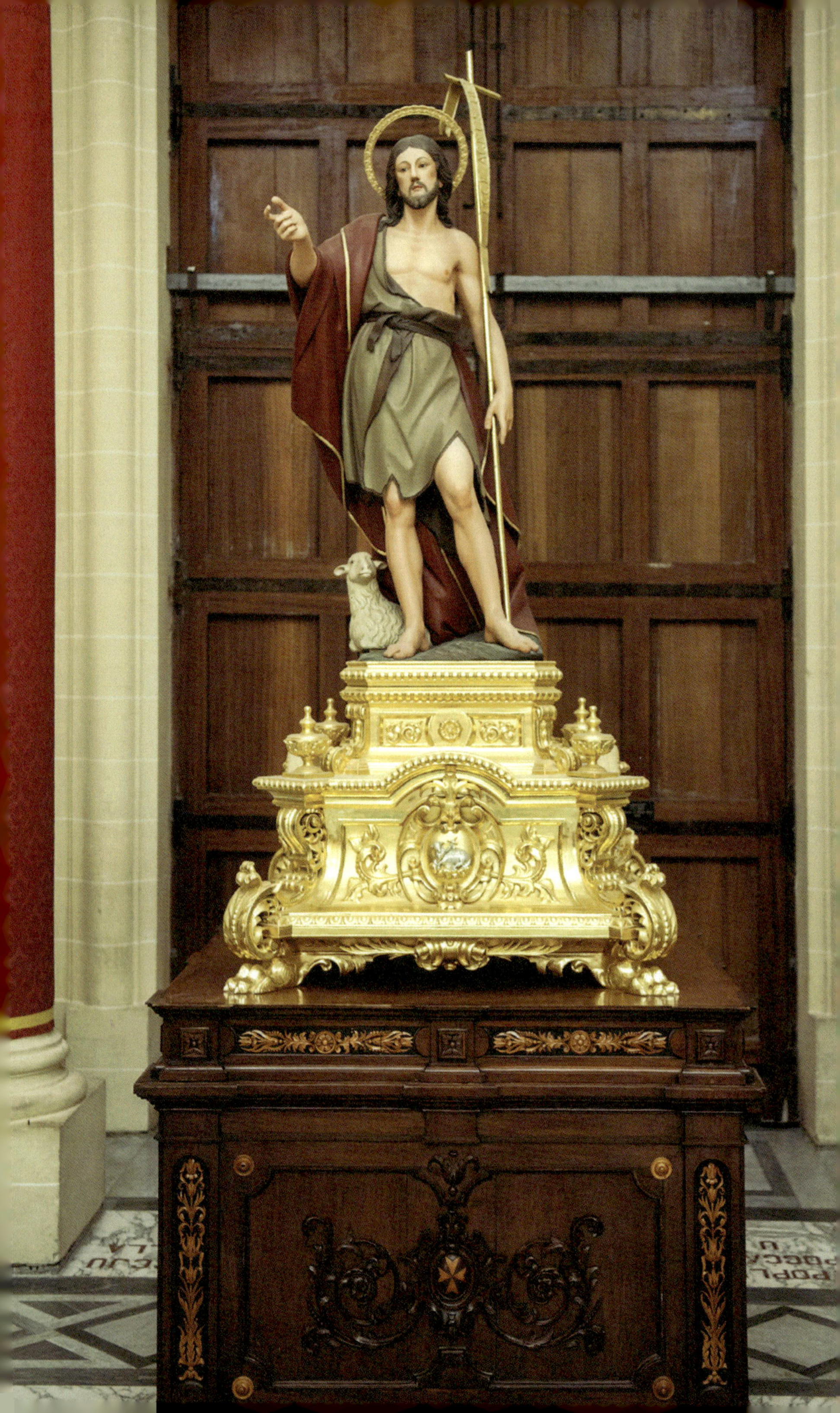

The titular statue of
St John the Baptist,
the Forerunner of
Christ, sculpted by
Pietro Paolo
Azzopardi (1845)
a student of
Mariano Gerada

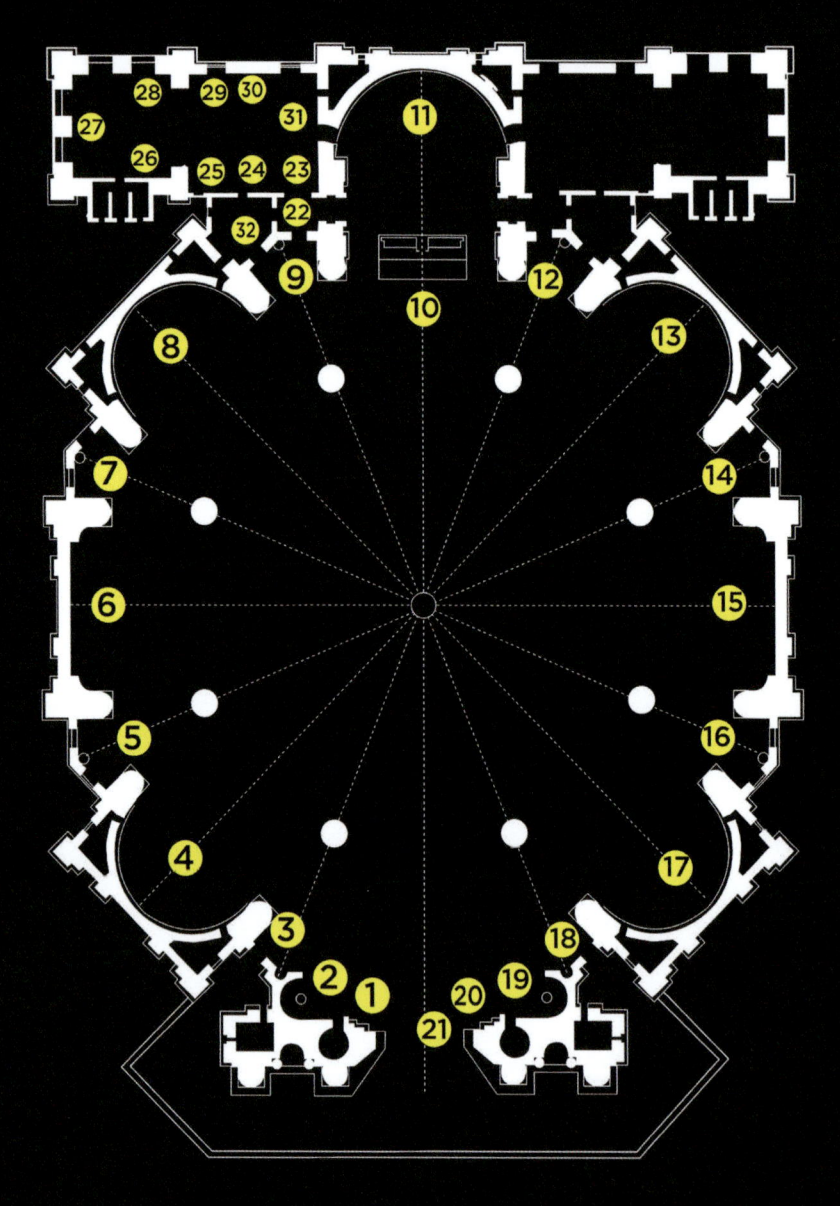

A GUIDE TO THE ROTUNDA

Printed in Poland
by Amazon Fulfillment
Poland Sp. z o.o., Wrocław

THE ROTUNDA
A TESTAMENT TO FAITH, COURAGE, AND LOVE